IDEA BREWS

THE CALLING

GEETHA VENKATARAMANI

INDIA • SINGAPORE • MALAYSIA

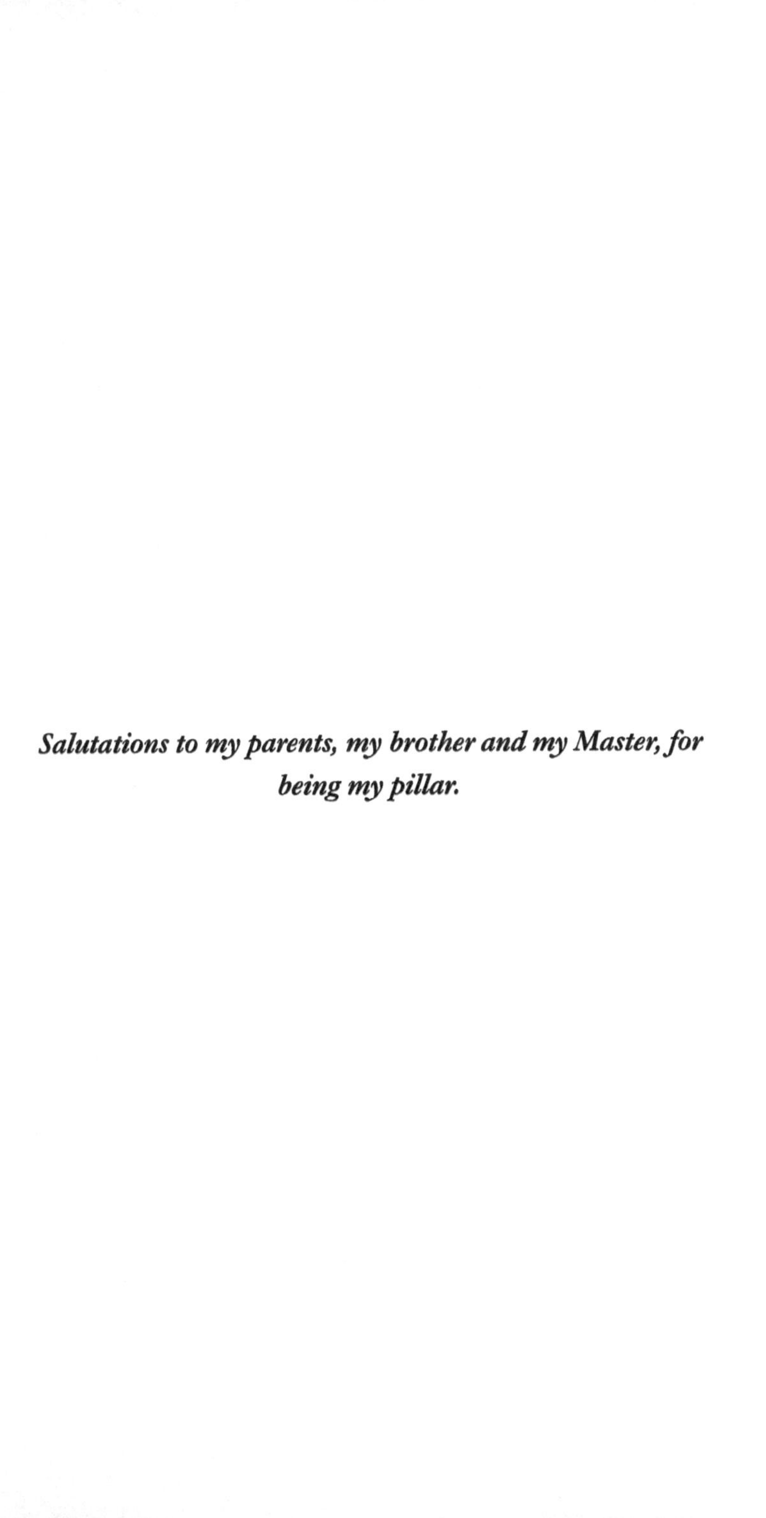

Salutations to my parents, my brother and my Master, for being my pillar.

When disagreements have a driving force,

What more to say of agreements?

Love and relationship are work-

Gratitude to you, make ease!

CONTENTS

GANESHA AND THE PUMPKIN

Ganesha is a young school-aged boy living in the town of Kailasa. One sunny morning, he woke up in his bed, feeling happy and playful. While brushing his teeth, he looked outside the window, wondering, "Wow, what a beautiful morning. What food would my mother cook today?"

Splashing his face with cold water, he paused for a moment. Opening his eyes and staring wide at nothing, he uttered in a loud, joyful tone, "Yellow pumpkin." Feeling delighted at his choice, he quickly finished his morning ablutions and rushed towards the kitchen. Little drops of water, still dripping from his seemingly excited face, wetted his shirt around the neckline and chest. Wasting no time, he quickly scanned through the vegetables placed in the storeroom and the refrigerator adjacent to the cooking area. To his disappointment, there were no pumpkins. He rushed towards the house garage. From among the vehicles parked, he boarded his bicycle, and wearing a helmet, he set off in search of a solution. The neighbourhood did not sell yellow pumpkins; it was probable that it had gone out of stock. To his eagerness, various pumpkin delicacies were haunting him. Ganesha was disheartened but couldn't give up his quest.

He introspected, "It will be so good to feast on some fine dishes that mother can prepare. But how so without pumpkins? Not quite possible. This is difficult. I cannot let go of the situation. It appears to be one of those rare occasions where I am forced to take matters into my own hands." He pondered how to solve the issue at hand. As he took it upon himself, he had to work hard to achieve his wish.

When one is determined and works hard with devotion to a specific goal, a way to succeed will emerge. Being receptive and open to embracing the challenge and sacrifice on the path, leads to success.

Ganesha purchased some pumpkin seeds from a neighbouring nursery and sowed them in his backyard.

Now this was his pet project. He wished to reap handsome quantities of yellow pumpkins. Even before the sapling could rise from Mother Earth's womb, he was making plans about the harvest: "One plant will bear many fruits, so I will reap many pumpkins at harvest. While I store some pumpkins for myself, the others I can give away to my friends and neighbours." He was delighted about his pumpkin project.

Thereon, he spent about an hour every day in the backyard and cared for the sown seeds. Lovingly, he would water the ground where the seeds were planted. Sitting beside it, he would finish his school homework and also recite loudly some verses from his study books. Not long after, a sapling appeared from the Earth. Ganesha was very excited at the sight of the young sprout. He began regular interaction with the plant, addressing it lovingly and treating it gently. He would inquire with the tender sapling, "Hope you are doing well and not bored alone here. Did you get adequate water and sunlight today?"

On another day, Ganesha played a musical instrument for the plant. He danced around the plant playing his favourite 'Damru.'

Days passed in a similar manner, and the sapling grew into a healthy creeper. A tiny pumpkin fruit appeared, and Ganesha's joy knew no bounds. A few more flower buds appeared. His hard work and patience were bearing fruit. He was overjoyed and showed his pet plant to his friend. Ganesha danced in joy and played the damru around the creeper. As time passed, the tiny pumpkin grew bigger and better. It was ready for harvest.

The next morning, Ganesha and his friend went to the backyard. His friend held a small knife in his hand. They both were excited to take home a big pumpkin. As they stood looking at the creeper, Ganesha thought to himself, "All these days, while I interacted with the creeper, there was no response from it. I know the creeper cannot speak, yet I wish to seek its permission before taking the pumpkin."

His friend spoke, "Come on, buddy, let us pick the pumpkin. It is big and fat."

Ganesha replied, "Let's ask the creeper for permission."

Friend: "What, are you mad? Plants do not speak. Let's take the pumpkin."

Ganesha: "No, my friend. Mother says we should not take anything that belongs to others without their permission. Let us seek the creeper's permission. If it does not reply, we can assume permission is granted." Both the friends giggled and stepped forward to do the needful.

To their surprise, the plant responded with a cry. Hearing the plant speak, Ganesha's friend screamed in fear, "What? Oh my god." Throwing the knife to the ground, he ran away. Ganesha too was shocked. Taken aback, he swiftly moved a few steps behind, away from the creeper. Still curious, Ganesha keenly watched the speaking plant in disbelief. His eyes, and mouth wide open. His breadth withdrawn, slow and deep. Hands spread away from the body and palms tightly clenched. While trying to grasp the event unfolding before him, a sense of fear gripped his pounding heart. It was a wild dream, watching a plant, as if woken from slumber, speaking and making sounds.

The plant opened its tiny eyes, looking at Ganesha, and spoke in a feeble voice, "Dear Ganesha, you have been kind and loving to me. I have enjoyed your immense attention and affection. It is through your support that I bear my fruits soon. Amazed by the power of your care, I feel blessed to have my baby pumpkins sooner rather than later. But now, while you want my fruit, I am very sad. I cannot grant you permission to part with my pumpkin. I am sorry. I hope you will understand as I only have my fruit. Please do not be upset, Ganesha," said the teary-eyed creeper.

Ganesha's teeth were grinding, and he felt mildly disturbed watching the unruly plant. From his glaring eyes, a tear trickled from one. He dared to observe and quietly listened to the whimsical speaker. His fists began to loosen, and the firm grip was easing. His breathing returned to normal, and he heaved a sigh of relief. Hearing the plight of the magical plant, Ganesha was confused. His natural reaction was to feel sorry for the creeper. He thus resolved not to pluck the fruit while waiting for the second pumpkin. The creeper thanked Ganesha for his kind consideration again, before closing its green eyes. All that transpired, left him wondering about the possibility of happy and sad feelings all around him.

Days passed in the same way as before. Ganesha would sing and dance around the plant. Eventually, a second pumpkin fruit appeared. Ganesha was very excited and jumped up and down in joy. Once again, holding a knife in his hand, he sought the plant's permission to take the second pumpkin fruit.

This time, the plant wailed in sorrow, tears flowing down its greenish eyes, and spoke, "Ganesha, if you take away my pumpkins, there will be nothing left of me. How can I live without my fruits? I am unable to bear the thought of separation from my pumpkin child."

The creeper expressed its grief and sought his support. Ganesha was sympathetic at heart and took pity on the creeper. By the influence of his positive thinking, he chose to be patient and let go of the second pumpkin. Preferring to wait for the third pumpkin's arrival, he hoped the creeper would give away the fruit, happily by its own will. Regardless of his prolonged wait to savour the delicious pumpkins, Ganesha was not perturbed and continued his merriment with the creeper and his friend. A third pumpkin arrived; it was close to being a well-grown fruit. After the day's routine, fun, and frolic in his backyard, Ganesha went home before evening. It was time.

During that night, there were strong winds and lightning. It was raining heavily. The downpour was intense, and water was logging everywhere. It seemed like the town was filled with rainwater up to a few feet. The ground was invisible, and the backyard was flooded. All things were either sinking or floating. The creeper was tightly holding onto its pumpkins. They were heavy, but the flowing water and wind speed caused the pumpkins to move and swing rapidly. Eventually, the pumpkins were torn away from the creeper, and the plant was in a bad condition.

Upon losing its fruits, the creeper sobbed and reflected to itself, "I was completely invested in bearing and nurturing my baby pumpkins. In spite of all my love and care, my fruits are gone. Snatched away by the rain and gusty winds. Neither could I enjoy their company for long nor could others relish my pumpkins. They are washed away, without any valuable use. Now I am lonely. All I did was to care about my own interests. Was it my selfishness that led to my pitiful condition? The time and efforts I spent, have become worthless…. My purpose was to bear fruits so everybody could eat them to build good health. People would have been happy and appreciated me. Nothing of that sort will happen to me anymore. I too have lost the purpose of my life. Now I am fruitless and directionless. Come morning, when Ganesha visits me, neither I nor my pumpkins will be present to greet him. Ganesha shall be so heartbroken, seeing me gone with my pumpkins. Maybe I am insensitive to think of only my happiness, without considering the effect of my choice on Ganesha and others around? I was misled by a few joy-filled moments, looking away from my larger life purpose. In spite of getting several opportunities to focus on my purpose, I unwittingly defeated my own glory." Tears flowing down, the plant closed its eyes and accepted all that came of it as the natural outcome of its own choices in the hands of the mighty nature.

Hearing the loud noise of the storm and rain, Ganesha woke up in the middle of the night. Seeing through the window, he could not notice much due to the darkness all around. He turned on the lights in his room and, carrying a torch, Ganesha rushed out to the backyard to check on the pumpkin creeper. To his utter shock, the plant was gone and nothing, but muddy water stood in its place. Ganesha looked around and found the plant floating away in the fast-flowing rainwater. While he knew that the rainwater collected around was headed to a nearby stream, he quickly ran after the drifting plant, guided only by the moving torchlight. He took a leap of faith and fell with a splash into the knee-deep muddy water. After much effort, he successfully grabbed the creeper and, mindfully picking it, he stood up. Running his torchlight up and down on the plant, he stood completely drenched & smeared in muck. The pouring rain washed the silt off his body. Managing himself on his way back, he rushed to his room. Checking on the plant under bright light, he noticed the roots were intact, but the pumpkins were gone.

Ganesha potted the plant immediately and prayed with folded hands for the plant's revival. Hoping for it to catch the sun's rays first thing in the morning, he changed into dry clothes and placed the pot by his room window.

The next morning, as soon as Ganesha woke up, he sat beside the plant and spoke sweet, soft words. He played his favourite damru while sitting beside it. The plant gently opened its eyes and apologised to Ganesha for having neglected him and not sharing its pumpkin.

It said, "Ganesha, I was being self-centred and did not think about your well-being. I was incorrect in thinking that all my fruits were mine alone. You have showered me with much love and care. Your attention has ensured I am always provided for and nurtured. It was due to my foolishness that I was holding only for myself, causing us both to face much trouble due to nature's fury last night. On account of my heavy pumpkins, I was torn away; else I would have still managed to survive by myself. Meanwhile, you too could have enjoyed delicious pumpkins, just as was the intended purpose of my creation."

Ganesha said, "I am very happy to see you getting better. You are my friend, and I respect your preferences."

Ganesha smiled and gently patted the plant.

The weather had settled, and the plant was again placed in the backyard. Following last night's event, Ganesha's friend came looking for the magical plant. They both continued to shower care and attention on the plant. Some days passed, and a tiny pumpkin appeared. As always, Ganesha rejoiced, danced, and played damru around the creeper.

As time passed, the fruit grew. The following morning, while Ganesha and his friend visited the creeper, they found a big pumpkin lying on the ground.

The creeper lovingly smiled at Ganesha and spoke in a soft tone, "Here is your gift. Thank you for loving and forgiving me."

Ganesha's happiness knew no bounds. He and his friend jumped up and down in joy. Ganesha hugged the pumpkin creeper and thanked it. His persistence ended with a sweet dish to his delight and a life lesson for the creeper.

Compassion is a progressive attitude

MONKEY ON THE BRANCH

Morning mist covered the hilly ranges of Kapibetta on the city outskirts. Numerous pockets of dense vegetation are found in the region. Climate and soil are conducive for farming a wide variety of plantations. The deeper parts of these pockets house various animals like monkeys, occasional leopards, serpents, scorpions and birds. One such densely populated area is the Kapibetta (the monkey hill) housing a large community of monkeys. This is the basis for an ongoing conflict between humans and the monkeys.

The monkeys are led by their leader, a seasoned adult named 'Kapiraj.' He maintains a special squad of trained adult members. Among several other activities, the trained group provides secure signals to their herd, ensuring quick communications pertaining to potential threats and imminent danger for one and all.

The group has several children, dependent on their parents for survival and well-being. The members are usually busy with their mundane activities, jumping across trees, playing pranks on fellow mates, fighting and squabbling over choices, preferences, and so on. Among such prevalent behaviour and temperament is a young adult monkey 'Aneya.' All through, she watches her kith and kin for most of the time, unaffected by their ways and mannerisms. She does not behave as her peers in the community. She is the chieftain's daughter.

Aneya often sits on top of a branch, watching her seniors and children making merry and engaging in cohesive activities. While Aneya is not perturbed, she is rather content by not joining the troop for active socialisation. However, the chieftain's partner and Aneya's mother 'Mati' is worried about her child's indifference. Mati often coaxes her daughter to accompany her peers and neighbours in various social activities. Mati wishes her daughter would make friends and actively participate in social engagements and so on. But Aneya is calm as always and not moved by her mother's concern.

Being the alpha, Kapiraj is often busy in his routine community duties and aware of Mati's expectation and her desperate attempts to motivate Aneya. On the other hand, Aneya is conscious of Mati's concern but lacks the motivation to oblige. On one such day, Kapiraj watches from a distance as Mati's attempt fails to convince Aneya, who is unrelenting. Infuriated at his daughter's insensitive behaviour, the chieftain decides to support Mati. Taking matters into his own hands, he engages his special squad member 'Biddu' for the task. Biddu is a well-built, strong, huge monkey.

One afternoon, while Mati is away fetching food for the family, Biddu coyly reaches Aneya out of nowhere and, with a brush of his hand, pushes her off the branch. Aneya is caught off guard and drops head straight towards the ground. Mati, who was observing all that was transpiring from a distance, drops her stuff on the way; taken by shock, she rushes towards Aneya in a bid to protect her dear child. In the course of Mati's act, she ravages through the nearby trees, and her body is bruised. Unaware of her bleeding wounds, she manages to secure Aneya from the free fall. Having landed her child safely on the ground, she furiously rushes towards Biddu. Slamming him against a nearby tree trunk. Biddu realises Mati's might, and in a bid to save himself, he quickly retraces his path.

A chase ensues between Biddu and Mati, the latter chasing the former, whose bid was to escape Mati's hold. Biddu, being quite the craftsman, evades Mati's attention and escapes into the vegetative lands on the outskirts.

Bruised and weakened, Mati withdraws from the brawl and returns to her abode. Aneya and a few others tend to Mati's wounds. Feeding her food and herbs for a speedy recovery.

On the other hand, the humans farming on vegetative lands grow angry beyond reason and restraint. They decide to rid their farms of the monkey menace. Small pits are dug at the end of their land, marking a tiny patch between their agricultural land and the dense forest. These pits are deep enough to store chunks of wood, dry grass, leaves, and other items as fuel. The intent is to keep them deep and, if necessary, ignite them to scare away the monkeys.

On the other hand, following the events transpiring inside Kapibetta, Kapiraj learns of the bitter spat between Biddu and Mati. In order to resolve this conflict, he reveals the intent behind Biddu's act. The monkeys learn of the chieftain's attempt to instigate his daughter to overcome her indifferent behaviour. Aneya is visibly shaken to learn of the reason behind the attack. The news causes a stir in the community. Kapiraj then declares Aneya bizarre and odious. The monkeys give up persuading Aneya.

As usual, Aneya spends days and nights watching her surroundings, sitting or sleeping on the same branch. Some members of the herd devised an effective plan to utilise the idle Aneya to their convenience. Monkeys, with young ones to be watched over, would leave their children with Aneya while running errands in the area surrounding Kapibetta. Aware of all that goes on around, Aneya does not object.

In hindsight, she maintains a watchful eye over the children around her on the tree branch. As time passes, a child named Vidyut bonds well with Aneya. While children play among themselves, Vidyut feels drawn towards the calm and reserved Aneya. Scratching and pulling on her, snuggling into her arms, and so on. Aneya does not protest Vidyut's behaviour; rather, she finds him amusing.

Weeks pass, and the harvest is almost ready. One evening, the farmers decide to act on the premise of curtailing a trail of recent mishaps. Anticipating uncontrolled monkey menace, the farmers light the fire pits on the outskirts. Sparks rise from the deep pits. A few guards are needed to ensure the fire burns well into the night. Till midnight, ensuring it does not turn out. Assuming all is well, they leave the pits to continue burning. The dry leaves and barks contained in these pits burn to full glory. They light up the whole surroundings, chasing away the darkness. It is a breezy night, and strong winds carry the burning leaves, and fire sparks further into the dense forest. These flying chunks stick and spread onto other plants and trees on the ground. A wildfire breaks out. Animals and birds panic and run back and forth in order to escape the flames and smoke. The fire is contained to Kapibetta.

Aneya, seated on the branch, notices from a distance the blazing flames and rising smoke high into the sky. The heat gets closer, gradually getting unbearable. The monkey chatter rises high, turning into howling and loud screaming all over. Birds take flight, and animals run around to protect themselves. The chieftain and his partner Mati are woken up by the loud noise and burning smell. Kapiraj, sensing the impending danger, announces immediate evacuation from Kapibetta. The special squad communicates a series of howling cries to pass on the chieftain's message. All begin to flee their homes. Their chase for survival is surrounded by complete chaos.

Mati requires rest but regardless of age, health and willingness all are forced to leave their world behind. Mati persuades Aneya to join her, while Aneya chooses to stay behind, insisting to pursue a rescue operation along with others of the special squad. She continues to guide the panic-stricken monkeys on a safe route leading beyond the outskirts of Kapibetta, to the dry lands.

To comfort Mati, Aneya assists her in crossing over a branch, passing over and above a marshy land. Within a few seconds, Mati trips off the branch. While attempting to hold Aneya, who is unable to grasp the culmination. Aneya watches in disbelief as the lag of a few seconds costs Mati her balance. The confusion in Aneya's eyes transforms into shock as she attempts to grab her falling mother from a death trap. Alas! Holding onto emptiness, tears roll down her terror-ridden eyes. Mati falls, and her loud screams become distant as she goes out of sight, heading straight into the marsh. Aneya looks around, desperate to catch a glimpse of Mati, staring into the blank. The dark events transpiring that night were more than anybody anticipated in the wildest of their dreams. All that was left for Aneya was the smoke-ridden air to inhale.

Aneya pondered as to what she could do best in the situation. She felt a thrust to her chest. Drawing her attention back to herself, she noticed a young child clinging to her. His eyes are wide open, pronouncing the fear of the unknown. It was Vidyut. He did not look as good as before. The naughty, happy kid was trembling and smeared with black soot all over him. His grip around her neck was hurting, and he was inconsolable.

Aneya went blank. Thoughts of Mati began to flood her mind. She then saw Mati sitting on a low-lying branch and telling, "I am fine. Now go on and help others in these dire circumstances." Aneya suddenly realised that Vidyut was still clinging to her. Glancing at Vidyut, she looked back towards Mati, who was nowhere in sight. It was all dark. "Was that really my mother? or am I hallucinating?" She questioned herself while drawing a long breadth. Looking at the child, she wondered "Mother is mighty, experienced and capable of caring for herself. The weak and incapable are the children and the old ones. I have to choose now: whom to protect?" It was getting hotter, and not another moment to spare for her loss.

Aneya ignored her inner turmoil, her emotions rising. Taking deep breaths and repeating to herself, "I need to help the needy who are reaching out to me. I should not forsake their lives to pursue my mother, who is probably on her own." She made a tough call. A voice inside her head said, "Forever, this will hurt me." Ignoring all that was pilling within her, she heaved a sigh at the unknown. Without further time to spare, she dove into action.

Aneya looked at the raging fire. It was closing in on them. She grabbed a few children by the hand and rapidly forged in the direction of the safe route. Hearing her safety calls, other flustered monkeys led by the chieftain followed the confident Aneya through a tunnel that lay hidden from sight between huge boulders. Through the dark blazing night, Aneya knew exactly which trees and boulders marked their safe gateway among the dense plantation of Kapibetta. As she led her herd away from the fatal fire, her heavy heart melted, and tears could not be held back.

The monkeys, other animals and birds that accompanied them through the safe route, reached farther beyond Kapibetta, all alive. Turning around to catch a glimpse of their lost home. They saw everything familiar to them was burning away like a haystack. It felt unbelievably painful. It was ghastly to have lost all they had. Amidst the ruins, standing by each other was their only hope and strength, in the face of the man-made tragedy.

Kapiraj's special squad took count of the rescued members of their community and concluded the evacuation to have been fully successful, with all community members safe. Hearing this, Aneya looked around to catch a glimpse of Mati, but failing to identify her, she broke down and cried inconsolably. Falling to the ground, she rolled like a child, as if battling an unbearable pain due to her separation from Mati. Biddu and Kapiraj approached Aneya and helped her up. In a bid to console her, they assured Mati's well-being and directed Aneya towards her mother. This time, she saw Mati sitting on the ground, looking exhausted but pleased.

Waving at Mati, Aneya's happiness knew no bounds. She ran to her mother, freed of all inhibitions as if nothing existed but only them. They hugged each other tightly while all the monkeys cheered and clapped for having survived the ordeal.

Meanwhile, Kapiraj addresses the crowd, "It has been a dreadful night. We did not anticipate the fire, chaos, and threat to our lives. Everything happened very fast, and nobody knew where we were headed or how to escape? We could not have survived all this if not for Aneya, who has guided us to safety. She took it upon herself to guide us through the safe passage. I applaud Aneya's presence of mind and calm behaviour all through this night."

Looking at Mati and Aneya, he said, "My community and I are ever so grateful to you. I am curious as to how you managed to perform this feat in a manner we witnessed you tonight?"

Aneya replied, "Father, over several months, I have explored Kapibetta and the dry lands we stand on, many times. Through observation and continued exposure to the landscapes, come my familiarity. Having roamed these day and night, it was possible to identify the safe route alongside the time and distance required for evacuation. Further, all the green routes were dangerous due to fire. The tunnel through the boulders was the only safe path of exit with the least of risks to our lives. The boulders acted as cover, preventing the flames. And with limited smoke entering the tunnel, we had a better chance of survival. On the other hand, I believe the squad could have responded better in dealing with the unwelcoming humans. The humans undertook several measures and succeeded in stopping us from venturing into their farms. While taking all they wanted at will from Kapibetta. We could not secure ourselves against their methods. Hence it wasn't for long before they wanted Kapibetta for themselves, and we were to be chased out."

The monkeys clapped for Aneya, and a loud howling roar sounded in the air as a mark of appreciation. The crowd cheered for Aneya in unison: "Excellent, we are proud of you."

Kapiraj's voice softened - "You are right, Aneya." His head lowered and eyes closed, he continued - "Forgive me dear child. Without understanding your perspective, I am at fault for judging your methods and underestimating you."

Aneya, rushed towards Kapiraj and holding his hand, replied, "Father. I was following in your footsteps but in a way suitable for my intellect and outlook. Your judgement gave me the freedom to explore my ways without any pressure or strings attached. In the end, as a family and community, we have looked out for each other. We all have been diligent; and so we stand together in the face of a fatal disaster. Like mother says, we should thank the almighty power that has shown us a way and kept us safe, than dwelling over the bygones."

Kapiraj smiled and swiftly raised Aneya's hand high above, announcing, "Now is our time. We will build our lives and shape a new future." All monkeys cheered and roared in unison, "Glory to our unity. Glory to the mighty power within us, that provides and guards all."

SLITHERING JOURNEY

It was a very hot summer. Rivers and large lakes began to recede at the water level, leaving behind their remnants as streams. The ponds had almost dried up. Rain was not foreseen in the near future. Thus, marking the onset of the drought period.

Long vacations meant trekking for Bhramar, a 30-year-old culinary artist. Apart from his college circle, he trekked with a group of like-minded individuals, whom he met through the city local networks for group escapades in hills and forests.

While the day was hot and torching, the night was bereft of coolness and breeze as though nature was motionless and withdrawn breathing. Bhramar had returned from a weekend forest trek and was quite happy bringing himself a gift from the hills. He placed a shoe box containing his personal gift in the room adjoining the kitchen. At the end of an exhausting day, Bhramar was fast asleep in his bedroom. Besides, Surekha, his partner, was tossing and turning.

It was midnight, and after much deliberation, Surekha began to drift into sleep. Time had passed, and Bhramar sat up on his bed. Turning to his left, he stood up and walked out of the room. Sureka was fast asleep by then. Walking to the kitchen, Bhramar opened the freezer and pulled out a tray. It was diced frozen fish. Picking a couple of frozen pieces, he headed to the stove, leaving behind an open freezer. Dropping them into a saucepan, he sprinkled salt and tossed the fish for a while over a stove that was switched off. Transferring the fish to a plate, he moved towards a corridor beside the kitchen. While he walked, his shoulder slammed on the open door, closing the freezer at once. The occurrence did not deter Bhramar. He slouched a few steps and then continued towards a room beside the kitchen. All the while, his eyes wide open.

Hearing the slamming noise, Sureka was awakened. Suspecting unusual activity in the house, she tried waking up the person beside her. To shake him up, she tried to feel the adjacent pillow. But found the spot empty, making her worried. She glanced at the clock beside the bed; it was half past three in the morning. Stepping out, she called him out discreetly. Rubbing her sleepy eyes, she peeked into the bathroom; it was unoccupied. Her suspicions grew. Perhaps it was Bhramar out there, she wondered. While unable to dismiss the possibility of an intruder, she remained in doubt. Mustering some courage, she picked a wooden walking stick placed in one corner of her bedroom by the wall. Swinging it wide across, she checked its power and swift movement. Slowly stepping out of her room, she turned on the lights in her path. Walking around the house, wheeling the stick in front of her.

An adjacent room door was open. She peeped in and noticed Bhramar standing, facing the wall. She was relieved. Placing the stick by the door, she watched him from behind. He was holding a plate to his left. As she walked towards him, Bhramar was opening a box with his right hand. From inside the box, he drew out the contents. Standing behind him and calling his name while rubbing her face with both palms. She saw him holding a grey colour shining rope to his right. Taking a closer look at the rope, she screamed in horror. It was a snake and not a rope.

Bhramar was shaken up by her loud cry, and so was the drowsy snake. Startled by the loud noise, he dropped the plate held to his left. The pieces of fish scattered over the floor, while the snake was repeatedly hissing. Sureka panicked, and so did the poor snake. She repeatedly knocked Bhramar's hand while shouting at him to drop the reptile. Before he could realise or react, by the force of her knocking, the snake was flung away from Bhramar.

Flying towards the window, it fell on the curtain drapes. Confused and scared, it quickly slithered in the direction of the breeze flowing through the window.

Bhramar was dis-oriented and looking around himself, could not recognise the surroundings. Sureka's only focus was on the dreadful snake. Watching it crawl out of the open window, she quickly shut the glass door after it. Taking deep breaths repeatedly, she was relieved at the reptile's exit from her home. "How did a snake come into our home?" she questioned in a trembling tone. Not hearing a word, she turned around, looking for Bhramar. He was lying on the floor, closed eyes, murmuring indistinctively. Approaching him, she patted his cheek vigorously, as if trying to revive him. All in vain, he was asleep. She checked his hands and face for unforeseen attack marks. There were no snake bites. Bhramar began to snore.

"Is he sleepwalking? This is so strange and out of the blue," she muttered. Surekha was visibly shaken.

Suspecting a human intruder and discovering a reptile was grossly wild. She sat on the floor beside him and watched over him for some time. It was four am by then. Feeling exhausted and emotionally drained, she no longer had the inclination to walk up to her bedroom or wake up Bhramar. Noticing the couch beside the door, she stretched on it. Lights were burning bright, helping her to stay awake and keep a close watch on her surroundings and Bhramar, who was fast asleep by then. Leaning on the couch, she eventually dozed off.

The snake was once again in the open, free, just like before its capture, in the shoe box. The dry climate left the snake feeling thirsty and hungry. It looked for food or at the least some water and shade, to sustain and protect itself from predators. It passed across hard concrete and muddy pathways. Careful to avoid open spaces and move under the shade of bushes and objects, all along to maintain a safe cover. After some travel, the snake came across the wetland and cow dung-smeared walls. He found a hole in the wall and passed through it. It was a shed.

It was half past three in the morning when Ramappa and Devappa sat down for a chat in the former's shed, that was adjacent to his cowshed. After several years Devappa, who hails from a village on the outskirts, came to visit his friend Ramappa in the city. Being childhood buddies, they spoke at length about their family affairs and dairy business. Carried away by their pep talk, Ramappa insisted they should warm up to a few drinks. They both occasionally consumed alcohol. While Devappa was accustomed to the village, toddy. Ramappa was used to the city's hard flavours.

Noticing a few cows to be awake, Devappa arose from his seat. Tying them to a short pillar and spreading grass for them to eat. He then walked back towards Ramappa. On a small table, there was a bottle of city liquor, a water jug, and two steel glasses. Eager to start, Ramappa served alcohol for them both. Sipping the drink, he was elated, as the beverage began to show effect. While Devappa was not at ease. He went slow on his first drink as against the intoxicated Ramappa, who was already on his fourth. Time passed, and it was half past four in the morning.

While listening to Ramappa's chatter, Devappa heard a familiar sound from somewhere nearby. He became suspicious and paid close attention as the hissing sound gradually became clear and prominent. Looking around, he noticed a large, dark-coloured snake slithering its way into the shed through a hole in the wall. Close to the hole was a corner stacked with piles of sacks against the wall. As Devappa watched keenly, the unwelcome guest slid behind the sack pile. It did not appear as if the snake moved beyond the corner. Devappa presumed the snake to have comfortably settled behind the pile.

Immediately, he alerted Ramappa. But his inebriated friend was in no state of mind to understand his warnings. Ramappa was wasted and could not follow Devappa's outright safety calls. Devappa understood that his friend was in no state to handle a crisis as this. He decided to manoeuvre the issue at hand. Devappa looked around and noticed some empty sacks hanging from a pole and a few sticks placed in another corner. He advised Ramappa to stay calm and not make any loud noise, so as to not startle the reptile. He picked a long stick that was curved in one corner and held a gunny bag. He slowly approached the pile of sacks with caution. Ramappa felt ignored and was annoyed at his friend's strange behaviour. He held Devapapa by his arm and questioned in a slurred speech, "What are you doing with my stick and bag? Are you stealing from me?"

Devappa was taken aback. Amazed by his friend's accusation, he frowned. Speaking in a dismissive tone, Devappa said, "No, the bag and stick are for catching the snake. It has sneaked into your shed and hidden behind this pile." he pointed the stick in the direction of the sack pile.

Ramappa, speaking in a slurred manner, "What? Snake! Are you stealing my snake?"

Devappa was frustrated but maintained composure, "What? shhh… speak softly. You will scare the reptile. Please sit on the chair and watch. Allow me to catch the snake."

Ramappa nodded his head vigorously, "It is my snake, I will catch it." saying so he tugged the bag off Devappa's hand.

Not surprised at his friend's rather aggressive behaviour, Devappa paused and thought to himself, 'Under the influence of alcohol, this man has lost his mind. It will be safer to leave, than watch him meddle with the snake. Diverting his attention is key to going home.'

Devappa replied, "Ok, here is your stick," handing it over to Ramappa. "Let me finish my drink before it's late," he remarked.

Hearing about the drink, Ramappa threw the stick and bag to the ground. Walking randomly, he tried grabbing the bottle placed on the table. Devappa held his hand and picked up the liquor bottle. As a bee to a flower, Ramappa was stuck to the sight of the bottle. Thus, Devappa led his friend out of the shed.

The snake was by itself, spending the rest of his night at the shed. After some time, Devappa returned to check on the snake. It was not behind the pile of sacks or in any corner of the shed. It was gone. After a careful check, Devappa presumed the snake had left for good. Retiring to his room that was adjacent to the cowshed, he caught up on his sleep.

The loud exchange of words between the friends had alerted the reptile. Sensing a looming threat, soon after their departure, the snake sneaked out of the shed. It followed the dim light burning in the nearby cowshed. Beneath the light was a tub filled with water. It was a hot summer, and a cow was drinking from the tub during the wee hours.

Noticing the approaching snake, it took objection and snorted at the reptile. The dry climate was unbearable, and the thirsty snake was desperate and chose not to stay away. Noticing the cow's opposition, the snake approached from the opposite side, but the cow wouldn't agree. He headed forward to stop the reptile and stepped on its body. The snake was hurt and, in a fierce reply, bit the cow on its limb. The animal was in pain and began to moo loudly. Disturbed by the series of events so far, the thirsty snake was petrified and headed out of the cowshed.

Enduring the pain caused from the animal attack, the poor snake slithered slowly across concrete pathways, trees, plants and muddy grounds. Carefully avoiding open space and maintaining cover of bushes and objects. A reasonable cover was essential to protect itself from potential predators. Spaces open to the sky were risky and needed close calculation before venturing. He came across tall grass and shrubs. It was comforting and restful after a tedious journey so far.

By the foot of a tree, under the cover of tall grass, screams from squirrels and mice were heard, running helter-skelter. The snake found mice to satiate his hunger and thirst. Noise from the ground drew the attention of a few big birds that were perched on the tree. A keen eagle closely observed, to ascertain the cause of the commotion. He noticed a prey on the ground, a snake. As if instantaneous, he swooped to the grass bed and picked the reptile by its paws while rapidly taking to flight. The snake was slithering hastily while being hunted. The quick movements of the prey enabled it to slip off the predator's grab, and the snake fell back to the ground.

Before the eagle could launch another attack, the reptile took cover under lush green bushes. The eagle waited to catch another glimpse of its prey while sitting on a branch. But the snake stayed put for the rest of the day. The intense chase, wriggling, and a fall from a height had left the reptile bruised and exhausted. He rested to recover his strength and carry on his pursuit for respite. Later, in the cover of dusk, he slowly moved beyond the shrubs, wounded and thirsty. The exhaustion caused by the dry weather made the passing difficult. He dragged himself looking for water or food.

Having crawled over concrete and hard surfaces, he found ease under heaps of dry leaves scattered on his way.

Finally stopping by a pile of rocks, he rested. Feeling his energy renewed under its cool shade, he wondered as a cool breeze blew by him. Raising his hood and watching the place around keenly. His sensory perceptions were strong and suggested a nearby source to conclude his pursuit.

It was nightfall, the time when most predators would retire for the day, and everything around would be getting quiet. Unable to decide on the right time to venture out, the snake stayed put. As time passed, it became dark. Looking in the direction of the breeze, a few ducks and swans fluttered at a distance. The snake was curious and watched the birds floating and swimming. He understood that not far from him, a waterbody lay. Feeling thirsty, he threw all his reasoning to the wind and set off slowly towards his final destination.

Moving with caution and very slowly, he was careful not to alert any potential predators around. Keeping a low profile and making his presence hardly felt, he slithered under the cover of darkness along the remnants of the park lying on the ground. Finally, he reached the banks of the lake, which was reduced by half of its water level. Small to medium-sized rocks were scattered around the water body. Taking position by these small rocks, he raised his body and looked right ahead. With a fully open hood, he beamed with joy as his long, tedious journey was to end now. He was ready to sink into the feeling of a sweet release that was to come. He crawled his way quietly into the water. The coolness of the water penetrated his skin, leaving him satisfied and a sense of being at home. He swam through the water for some time, quenching his long yearning for respite. Contended for the night, he found peace within himself!

Regaining his strength, he looked around, feeling pleased. Choosing to live by the lake, as he would face no shortage of food and water for this dry season. As he was making plans about his next stop, he felt being grabbed and lifted above the water. Finding himself flying far away, he looked above to realise it was an owl carrying him. Perhaps his final respite drew the owl's attention. It flew down and grabbed the snake by its beak.

The snake's inner struggle to thrive concluded on a joyful note, but his external struggle for survival continued. The owl flew away, pleased to have caught a wholesome meal.

WHERE DREAMS ARE SKY HI!

It was the rainy season, time for heavy downpour, deserted sky, wet grounds and crowded tree nests. A huge banyan tree stood in a big yard. It housed several bird families. The canopy form of the branches was a perfect nesting ground for sparrows and crows among other animals. In one of these nests lived a three-member sparrow family, consisting of mother, father and a baby sparrow.

The baby sparrow and his parents lived in the lower branches of the banyan. The baby's favourite activities were hopping around, eating, and flying with his friends to explore new places for fun and play. He would regularly undertake long flying trips with his friends for the thrill of it. On one such occasion, while flying back home, the baby noticed a huge tree. There were several of them in close proximity. He hadn't been there before. It was already evening, and the sparrow troupe decided to return the following morning to explore the Arjuna tree groves.

The next afternoon, the baby sparrow with his regular flock flew over to the grove. They spent time hopping, climbing, and playing in the water, eating fruits, seeds, insects, and all that they could find in the grove. As evening approached, there was a heavy storm and a sudden downpour. The banyan was not far from the Arjun grove. But the heavy rains made it impossible for the sparrows to make an emergency departure and return home to the banyan. So, the flock of sparrows took shelter in the Arjuna trees. The canopy was thick, and little water was passing through the dense structure.

Baby and a few of his friends could not stay put and continued to play. They began to climb one of the tall trees. After reaching mid-way, the deserted sky was clearly visible from a few branches to the inhabitants of the tree. Out of nowhere there was still one bird flying. Baby sparrow noticed this unique phenomenon. He admired big birds with big feathers. He stared at the single bird with large wings soaring high above, facing no hindrance from the pouring rain.

Baby wondered, 'Was the bird flying drenched in the rain, or was it even possible for it to fly above the rain clouds?' Called upon by his busy friends, he continued the climb with his companions.

At once, the rain stopped, and the flock regrouped on the ground by the tree trunk. They all flew back home to the banyan tree. All along, the baby was looking towards the sky, trying to catch a glimpse of the lone soaring bird.

Days, weeks, and months passed. Our baby sparrow had grown into a strong young sparrow. He would often spend time admiring the vast sky. His sight would search to behold the unique phenomenon that he once noticed. He was never over it. He held its memory as dear to himself. As he grew, his curiosity for the big bird grew, transforming from admiration to aspiration. Sometimes, he would be lost watching a big one soaring high in the sky.

That evening, his mother served him food, but our young sparrow was preoccupied with thoughts of the big winger.

Mother enquired, "Is the food not tasting good, baby? What happened?"

The young sparrow glanced at her and grinned to himself. Turning around, he continued to stare at the sky. Pointing in the direction of the lone big bird flying far away, he questioned, "Mother, who is that?"

His mother, looking in the pointed direction and narrowing her eyes for a clearer view, replied in a concerned tone, "Well, I can't tell from here."

"Hmm, father must know. I will check with him." remarked the young sparrow.

It was late evening. Wings held behind his back, young walked from one corner of the branch to the other, lost in deep thoughts and with a stern face, awaiting his father's arrival.

Mother sparrow watched her child's restless behaviour and grew worried for him, "What has gotten to my little one?" she thought. Meanwhile, the father flew back to his nest. Looking concerned, he hugged Young and his mother at once. Further instructing them to stay within their home for the next few days until a problematic situation subsided outside their home. Both Young and his mother were unable to follow the reasoning, leaving them confused.

Young had been patiently awaiting his father's return and could no longer withhold his excitement. Digressing from the issue being discussed among the family, he jumped in to start a new conversation by interrupting his father.

Grabbing the opportunity, he spoke hastily, "Agreed father. Now can you please tell me who that bird is, flying high in the sky?" he enquired.

Father was smitten by his child's curiosity and obliged, "How did the bird look, my dear? There are many of them out there."

Young added, "The one flying in circles alone and farther beyond other birds."

Father thought for a while and replied, "Maybe the eagle. It lives on the top branch of a nearby tree. I have been worrying about the eagle. There has been an unfortunate incident with the big bird. Its nest, along with the eggs, are gone missing. Both the parent eagles are fiercely searching. I heard they are even hunting down any potential miscreants. This is a dangerous threat to other birds. They seem to be quite furious and in a frenzy."

The father placed one wing on the mother's shoulder and gently tapped on the young's cheek with his other wing, while he spoke in a warm tone, "Avoid any risk to you both, please restrict your movements to our tree and not step beyond our home for the next few days."

Nodding her head in agreement, the mother spoke in a sympathetic tone, "Oh, the poor eagles."

Young did not gather much regarding the eagles personal loss. Later in solitude, he probed her, "Mother, what if the eagles lost their eggs and nest. They can always get another one, right? Why are these birds acting crazy?"

Mother replied, "Hmm…Young, if we lost our family, how do you think you would feel?"

Young replied, "I will cry and get it all back."

Mother explained, "Yes, that may be what the eagles are doing. We cannot know."

Young, "But I do not follow. Why should we stay home and not step out? We should actually console the crying eagles and help them find their little ones. Instead, we are …"

Mother Sparrow abruptly interrupted, saying, "Console? Did you not hear your father speak? It is the eagle we are talking about, not another sparrow. We all are afraid of them. They are deadly and will feed on us for their food."

Hearing his mother's words, Young kept quiet and was lost in deep thought, "The eagle can soar very high as if all the sky is his own. I wish to fly as an eagle. It will be so much fun…" He looked up at the star-studded dark sky, and a smile appeared on his face.

Looking at his own wings, back and forth, he muttered to himself, "My wings are small yet proportionate to my body weight and height. The eagle's body is big, and so are its wings. The eagle has to use a super-flying technique. If I can manage learning the eagle's technique, I, too, shall fly high in the sky." He was happy at the idea. But then his mother's warning flashed through his mind, "Oh, but the eagle can kill me too. Then what will be the point of all this? How would I learn from the eagle without harm to my life? What if I never get to fly so high?" wondered the baffled young sparrow.

While staring at a distance and quietly reflecting, Young resolved, "I need to solve this problem first. But how?" he wondered quietly, wearing a concerned look on his face.

He spent all the time analysing his situation from various perspectives, trying to find a practical way to engage the eagle to train him. The hurdle was not to be eaten. He spent nights unable to sleep while bathing in the beautiful moonlight. One such night, while young was quietly reviewing his situation and trying to identify a reasonable fix, his father's words flashed across his mind over and over again. After careful consideration, it suddenly occurred to him that his father had already settled his problem by hinting at the solution. He stood up and drew a map of how he could execute his plan. Eagerly awaiting the dawn, it was the most exciting night of his life. Little did he know what the morning had in store for him.

It was dawn and young was up, looking around curiously. Father called him for breakfast. Young grabbed his food and quickly gulped it up. Seemingly hungry, his father served him a second portion. But young being full, dismissed the kind offer.

His father coaxed him, "Why gobble food? You could relish it slowly. You seem hungry or in a hurry. To stay strong and energetic, wouldn't you eat well?" - he commanded.

Hearing all the questions, young obliged and ate the second portion, but not without protest. His parents were pleased, "We could have more such pleasant mornings." his mother remarked.

Ignoring all that was being said, he sat in a corner, staring at the sky. Noticing his disinterest in the family conversation, his father approached and stood beside him. His mother clasped her wings across her waist and spoke, "Young, who are you searching in the sky? Is it the eagle?"

Hiding his intent, he replied with a smile, "I like watching birds fly. Aren't we staying indoors?"

His mother nodded in agreement, saying, "OK, we are going to pick some twigs with aunt Sparrow around here. We will be back soon. Will you be fine?"

"Yes, Mother," confirmed Young in an overenthusiastic tone. He then continued watching the sky, and his keen eyes were pleased at the sight of the same eagle in the sky. It was time.

Young Sparrow, skipping the onlooker's view, flew towards the grove not far from the banyan. He landed on the grounds of the Arjuna grove and hopped around for a while looking for something. He did not find anything out of place or different. He then flew to the lowest branch and began climbing up a tree while inspecting the surroundings for any trace of the missing nest. As he reached the higher-level branches, he found an empty nest open to the sky. He went around mid-level branches and found a pit-like formation with a few branches entwined. After all this hard work, he was hungry. Looking around for food, he pecked at a few fruits of the Arjuna. In one corner of the branch, there lay a couple of eggs without a nest, stuck in a hole. He flew around and inspected them. Finding no other nest in the vicinity of the tree, he presumed them to be off the eagle. It was already a bright, sunny afternoon, and Young flew to the top part of the tree. The eagle had returned and perched on the empty nest with closed eyes.

At the sight of the big bird, the sparrow's heart skipped a beat. Watching the bird's physical features, Young knew of no measure to compare. The bird's vibrant colour, curved beak, sharp talons, huge, feathered body, and wide wings were striking. He was transfixed by the sharp hunter, unable to look away from the sight he beheld. He observed the bird's sheer appearance, and a sense of fear swept over him.

The thought of seeking this giant to help him seemed like an implausible feat. Self-doubt seeped into his mind. He wondered, "Is my plan far-fetched? Am I brave or stupid?" Perhaps reality began to sink in. In a flash, he recollected all that he wished to learn from the eagle.

Young mumbled, "The dangerous part of my plan is to help the eagle find its eggs. Now, to draw his attention towards me… hmm." Raising his brows and shaking off the thought, he laughed in his mind's voice, "Hehehe…" Replaying the same repeatedly in his mind left him feeling bitter in his mouth.

He paused and quietly reflected, "Is all this really worth doing? Should I risk my life to fulfil my passion? What if I am eaten by the scavenger?" He stared at the scary sight ahead of him, as if the bird would fetch him all the answers to take him forward. As he looked on, his attention was drawn to the vast sky that lay beyond the eagle. The backdrop of his struggle drew him away from all the tension that was driving him to the brim. The serene appearance of the sky ignited his desire to soar high again. Perhaps, all else was only a staged performance to culminate in the epitome.

He continued, "Flying high is a part of me, and without this, I am incomplete." Taking a deep breath, he reflected, "Having pursued this goal for so long with sleepless nights and sacrifices, having come this far, I cannot abandon my strive now. I cannot lose my mojo. This is my joyful purpose and dream. Do or die, I am going for it." His eyes fixed on the blue sky. He cleared his head and gained momentum to move forward. Taking a leap of faith, Young decided to engage with the eagle and lead it to the discovered eggs.

Taking note of the mighty bird on the branch, Young flew towards it, like a moth to a flame. He then fluttered and chirped around his subject. His ignorance drew him to the ways of hell.

Disturbed by the continuous tweet, the big bird opened its eyes and found nobody. Turning in the direction of the noise, it saw the tiny rascal deliberately drawing its end, making a hue and cry.

The eagle thought, "What an amusing prey. Calling out to me... for what? Hmm... I am bored, and so is he. Must be wishing an end to his pitiful life," and chuckled.

Stretching its wings and standing straight, the big bird took a stern account of the uninvited guest. Judging the time to be right, Young quickly flew with all his might away from the beast, and with the eagle after him, a chase ensued. The sparrow's route was rather puzzling. Instead of flying away, he waited for the eagle at one branch corner, putting himself through a dire circumstance. Noticing the bird approach, Young fluttered around a pit and continued to chirp at the eagle. Surprised at the sparrow's death dance, the eagle rushed to grab the poor fellow in a single bite. Young managed to sneak below the entwined branches and stared at the eagle, watching from a distance. The eagle flapped its wings, looking for ways to catch the prey. While forging ahead, it glanced at something familiar beneath its large feet. It paused and stared hard into the pit. Taking cognisance of the unexpected, it reviewed its content… few eggs. There were its beloved eggs.

The sparrow rose up again into the air and chirped at the wonderstruck eagle. The big bird grabbed the eggs and flew back to its nest. Having settled them safely onto its own, the eagle looked at the sparrow strangely.

"I was surprised by your odd behaviour from the start. Your attempt to disturb and direct me towards the corner of a branch did not seem natural but rather a planned act. Now that I have found my eggs, should I conclude that you helped me locate my lost eggs?" demanded the eagle in a stern tone.

Young replied, "Yes, my friend. I was trying to help you."

The eagle looked keenly at the tiny bird. "Hmm… friend you say!" in a moderate tone.

The eagle continued, "Thank you for the kind consideration. No bird in your class is a friend of mine. We are the predators, and you are the prey. That is natural to all of us. But you stand out from your lot. Your courage reeks of audacity, and your will is as tall as the sky. I presume that for a bird of your valour, you must be ambitious too. So tell me, what brings you to visit me, for I can also be your end?"

Young replied, "Yes, all that you said is accurate. I have come looking for you. I admit you are not to blame if you choose to hurt or eat me. It shall be well within your natural behaviour. But what I did today is well beyond my natural behaviour. I hope you could follow my lead. My class of birds fears you for their life, while I, on the other hand, admire you…"

The eagle interrupted, "You admire me? It makes no sense. Why would I believe that?" he mocked.

Young continued, "I see you as the means to achieve my dream. I am fascinated by your flight skills. I wish to soar high in the sky and have seen you do it. If I fear you, how else could I upskill myself? I am here to seek your help. Can you please teach me the flying technique to soar high above the clouds?"

The eagle laughed loudly. "Can you…? Believing you could ever fly like me is preposterous. I thought you were an intelligent bird when you found my eggs. But you have lost sight of reality. Have you looked at yourself? You must have seen other sparrows and eagles. Can there be any comparison between the likes of yours and mine? Don't you recognise how entirely different we are?"

Staring hard into the sparrow's face and in an authoritative tone, the eagle added, "I am the king with large wings, and my body is made for high flight. On the other hand, you are a tiny bird and not built for flying high, let alone for a stomach full of food. I am sorry to disappoint you, but your dream is pointless."

Hearing this, Young was disheartened, and his feelings showed on his sad face. He wondered, "Either the eagle does not wish to teach me, or he is telling the truth. How should I know the truth?"

He spoke in a low tone, tears welling up in his tiny eyes. "Do you think teaching me is a waste of time, or that I am not worthy to fly like you?"

Hearing these words, the eagle softened its tone and replied, "You belong to my food group. Since you have bestowed much happiness upon me by finding my eggs, I haven't harmed or eaten you yet. Instead, I respect you and am, therefore, behaving with restraint. Trust me, friend, I speak the truth."

With tears rolling down his face, Young began to sulk with his head lying low. He was heartbroken and inconsolable. The eagle found this sight rather disturbing to watch, and to his own surprise, he decided to please the young sparrow.

He said, "Dear sparrow, there is one way you can still fly high like me."

Hearing this, Young looked up with hope in his eyes and a curious look on his face.

The eagle added, "Trust me, I will keep you safe. Follow my instructions. Will you?"

Young nodded in agreement, tears of joy flowing down his face.

The eagle continued, "That's like my friend. Come hop on to me and grab me tight."

Young did just as he was told. The eagle carried his new friend on his back and soared high above. They flew above the clouds, cruising at high altitudes together.

The young sparrow actualised his dream, achieving a feat no other small bird could. He flew higher than the eagle in the vast open sky. Young was extremely happy. The eagle, too, found his friend's company surprisingly pleasurable.

A new day, a new bond in the rarest of associations, where courageous intellect can break barriers. Built on the grounds of compassion and humility, determination and dedication, hard work and courage.

Dreams are Sky High!

THREE GOOD FRIENDS

Vidya Kendra is a higher secondary school situated at the heart of the capital city of Bengaluru. It is well known for imparting good culture, academic, and extracurricular engagements for the students. Sameira, Pratha, and Meera are three friends studying in the ninth class. The annual day programme of the school is around the corner, and all students are gearing up for the upcoming event.

Pratha, is a go-getter. Meticulous about all that is hers. Her clothes, food, and friends are all chosen consciously. Sameira is bubbly and charming, a daydreamer yet assertive. Meera is sharp and observant. She knows her priorities and can stay focused. What keeps them together are their hearts.

During class breaks, the friends eat and play together. Sameira is eager about the upcoming programme and is planning their performance. "I think we should do a fashion show. What do you gals say?" She questioned Meera and Pratha.

Pratha was pleased at the idea of getting dressed up. She approved of it and was excited to join her friends. "Sounds fun. We need several fancy clothes. Do you think we should buy specific ones for the show?"

Meera's intent was to reason. "A fashion show, is it? Hmm, flaunting our getup, walking around the stage to some jazz. Shall we do more than that? How about a dance performance?" she asked suggestively.

Sameira replied, "Everybody will dance. Fashion shows are different. We can hire a makeup artist and wear some real fancy attire and footwear. You know, my sister Sahara bought these branded sandals from 'Ikar' last week. They are awesome. They light up and shine while walking. Imagine as we walk the ramp, we will look fantastic in our outfits, with a spotlight on our feet. We will rock the show."

All three giggled among themselves. Smitten by the idea, Pratha said, "Tell us more about the sandals."

Sameira said, "Wait till you see it. Sahara says they are very classy. They are transparent, embedded with a single line of crystals along the entire footwear. As you walk along, light beneath the crystals turns on, and the brightness is multi-coloured by the crystal reflections. It is truly a beauty beyond words. One has to see it. You both should buy 'Ikar' sandals. We three will look fab and super classy wearing them. I can already imagine us three walking together like goddesses," she said. Her face lit up and eyes beaming in excitement.

Hearing all this, Meera and Pratha screamed in excitement. Sameira too joined them. Other students eating and playing nearby frowned at them in distaste and disbelief. While some others smiled back, watching them happy. Realising they were on school premises, Pratha and Meera regained their composure, while Sameira continued her loud excited talks. To calm Sameira, Pratha drew her close and pushed her chin up, signalling her to stop.

Smiling at Pratha's act, Meera whispered, "I want to try them. How much do they cost?"

Sameira whispered back, "About 15k. But totally worth it. Wait till you see them."

Meera asked, "Wow, 15k? It must be very good. Show us the picture." She insisted, "You must have already worn them. How do they feel?"

Sameira replied proudly, "No, Sahara did not allow me to even touch them. I'm going to try them today, though."

Pratha asked, "But how will you? Sahara…."

Sameira chuckled. "While she is away. She will be gone for her karate classes this evening, and I am skipping mine. So, the sandals are all mine to try." As she narrated her plan, she was all sorted and on cloud nine.

Meera almost shouted excitedly, "Woo hoo! that sounds like a plan!" The three girls had a hearty laugh and hi-fived each other over the break.

Lunch break was nearing end, and Pratha began to feel restless. While Sameira was speaking, Pratha would repeatedly check her wristwatch. Meera observed Pratha's behaviour for a while.

Watching her growing restlessness, Meera held her palm and enquired, "Are you okay? You look worried. Is there a problem?"

Sameira, who was talking non-stop, suddenly snapped at Meera, "I'm still talking, please don't interrupt. Wait for me to finish."

Meera replied, "Pratha does not seem fine. See the tension growing on her face?" She then cajoled Pratha into sharing her concern.

Sameira observed Pratha. "What happened, Pratha? We are discussing our annual day performance. There is a lot to prepare. What else is bothering you?"

Pratha, confused and worried, said, "Gals, mathematics class is in the next 10 minutes, and my homework is not done. I planned to finish it during lunch break. But in between our discussion, I have missed. Wonder what's in store for me. Today is a bad day."

Sameira checking her watch, "You still have 8 minutes before the class starts." Handing over her notebook, she added, "Here. Now, quickly copy my work and walk into the class a few minutes late. Just make an excuse that you are feeling unwell. You should be fine. Yeah?"

Meera replied, "Yes, let's help you finish the homework." She opened Sameira's book and added, "If we both help her finish her assignment, she won't be late for the class."

Sameira said, "Come on, Meera. Miss Lily will easily identify differences in our handwriting. Only Pratha should write; otherwise, she will be in trouble again."

Pratha said, "Yes, Sameira is right. You gals go. I will finish the work and join you both in the class soon."

In the classroom, it was ten minutes past and the students happily chatted while awaiting Miss Lily. Pratha rushed in, blurting out her practised lines, "Excuse me, ma'am, may I come in?" Students watched Pratha, and some spoke in chorus, "Yes, you may," followed by loud laughter. Miss Lily was nowhere in sight. Pratha was relieved to join the class before the teacher's arrival. She walked in feeling glad, as if winning an award.

Taking her favourite spot, the seat between Sameira and Meera, she looked pleased. They continued discussing the sandals and how it was a lucky day for the latecomer.

Shortly, "Shush… shushing" resonated in the air, spreading across the room, followed by a wave of momentary silence. The students stood up in their respective seats and greeted Miss Lily in chorus, "Good afternoon, ma'am." Meera sneaked a peek at her watch and remarked, "twelve minutes late." Hearing this, all three girls giggled.

Miss Lily greeted the students and looked pleased. In a sweet, joyful tone, she asked, "Has everyone completed the homework?"

"Yes, ma'am," resounded in the class.

"Anybody not finished, stand up, please."

Seeing none, Miss Lily remarked, "Very well. Give yourself a loud applause," clapping loudly. As the assignments were submitted on time, the students joined the teacher and clapped for themselves and each other. The clapping would go on for a full minute. There was noticeable improvement in student performance. Miss Lily started the ritual of student appreciation, possibly to boost their morale.

She added, "We have a class test next Monday, covering chapters completed so far. Please come prepared; you have a week's time.".

In the evening after school, Sameira and Pratha headed to the school parking lot. They boarded the school bus adjacent to the gate. Seated behind each other by the window, they continued chatting with Meera, who was standing outside the bus. She looked at her watch and commented, "ten minutes late." Meanwhile, an all-black stylish sedan stopped by the gate and honked once. Watching the car arrive, Meera abruptly stopped the conversation and waved at her friends, "Okay, gals, time for me to go. See you tomorrow. Bye," she smiled. As she walked away, her friends watched her with envy. A lady chauffeur stepped out of the car and opened the back door for Meera.

Pratha said, "Look at the driver's saree. It is so well draped. Does she iron it after draping? I have never seen anybody's saree so perfectly in place."

Sameira said, "No, man. I think it is stitched that way. Looks like a ready to wear. Watch her hair; it's always tied up into a bun. So boring to see the same styling every day. I wonder if she ran out of options. We can teach her some styling..."

Pratha said, "That may be her uniform." They both smiled and nodded in agreement. Meera's car started and picked up speed as it drove away.

Sameira said, "Meera is so lucky. She has her own luxury car and a personal driver, while we commute by bus. She has such a wonderful life."

Pratha said, "Of course, she is super rich. Her room must be huge, with a lot of clothes and other matching accessories. "

Sameira said, "Yeah, I hope she will buy great gifts for our birthdays too." On that note, both burst out laughing and hi-fived each other on their way back home.

Every morning, students assemble at the school playground for prayer, followed by quick warm-up exercises, while standing in parallel lines. Towards the tail end of a line, the three girls were standing in the sequence of Pratha, Sameira, and Meera. The warm-up was getting difficult for Pratha. Stepping back, she leaned towards Sameira and whispered, "I'm feeling sick. Do you have a sanitary napkin?"

Sameira looked around for a teacher but found none. She then pulled out a zipped pack from her bag and handed it over to Pratha. "Here, take it."

Grabbing the pack, Pratha walked away towards the school building. Watching her go, Meera leaned forward to inquire with Sameira, "Where's she going? she probed in a surprised tone"

Sameira said, "Washroom."

Meera asked, "Oh, what happened?"

Sameira replied, "Menses, I think."

During lunch break, Pratha asked, "Sameira, can I borrow another pad?"

Sameira replied, "Oh, I only had one. Sorry."

Pratha said, "No worries." She then enquired with Meera. Who handed her a silky packet. That afternoon, before heading home, Pratha spoke to Meera, "Thank you, dear. Your sanitary pad is very nice. It's super comfortable and no complaints at all. It's indeed an amazing product. I haven't seen these before. Where do you get them?"

Meera smiled, "I know it's very good. It's not a regular brand and is available only in elite stores. My mum buys it from a select outlet."

Pratha said, "Oh, I see. Sounds luxurious and feels great. Can I borrow one?"

Meera smiled, "Sure. You really seem to like this. Don't you?"

Pratha giggled, "Yes, I would love to borrow from you every time." Meera chuckled and nodded in agreement. Sameira watched all this and offered to Pratha, "You can borrow from me too."

Pratha was quick, "Thanks. I use the same brand. I want to try Meera's; it's so much better. You should try too." she asserted.

Sameira felt a pinch. Watching their bond grow, she felt a resentment within.

A few days passed, and it was Pratha's birthday. Celebrations were at Pratha's home. Invitees were a close circle of family and friends. Sameira and Meera looked their best at the party, while Pratha was gorgeous. After the cake-cutting ceremony, Pratha was showered with gifts. As Meera handed a gift to Pratha, Sameira recollected their bus conversation, referring to expensive gifts from Meera. She signalled Pratha, raising her brows and smiling wide. Pratha was pleased in anticipation of an expensive gift from Meera. She treated the package fondly and carefully placed the gift in a secure spot. The party was over, and Meera headed back home. Sameira stayed back to help open the gifts.

One by one, Pratha opened many gifts and explored the new articles. Next was Meera's package. Tearing through the fancy wrap, underneath she found a box of 'Elite' brand sanitary napkins. It contained orange-coloured small silky packets of individual napkins.

Pratha paused for a moment and spoke slowly, "Wow, my favourite napkins," nodding in acceptance. Sameira was taken aback. Picking up a few silky packets from the box, she looked back and forth at them, analysing the gift. Holding a packet, she pointed it at Pratha and spoke in a bitter tone, "Sanitary napkins for a birthday gift? What is wrong with Meera? This is not something to be gifted to a best friend," Sameira chuckled.

Pratha was confused by Sameira's reaction. Drawing a deep breath, she spoke, "Hmm… (pausing…) is it bad for an expensive one too?" she asked inquisitively.

Sameira replied, "Of all the special gifts that Meera can afford, she chose sanitary napkins for you? This is inappropriate. You should tell her this."

Pratha's joy of owning her favourite brand of napkins vanished, and in its place, she sounded sad. "So, this is bad… is it?" She sought Sameira's validation.

Sameira asserted, "Of course, this undermines you. It means you cannot buy a good sanitary napkin."

Pratha said, "But Meera knows this is my favourite. And my mother also refused to buy me an expensive brand. She says it's unnecessary and a waste of money."

Sameira said, "Yes, this gift is unnecessary. You deserve a beautiful gift. Imagine, when people ask you what gift you got, will you show Meera's gift to others? No, right? Because it's a bad gift, and you have to hide it from others. No doubt."

Pratha said, "That's not the point, Sameira. I told Meera I am fond of this, so maybe she got it for me."

Sameira said, "No. This gift means she has ignored you. Meera simply took out a new pack of sanitary napkins from her cupboard and wrapped it for you. I was hoping she would show her appreciation through a beautiful gift. Didn't you have hopes for a special gift? Now I feel bad for you."

Pratha: "It's fine. I have something that I like; let's just leave this topic." Pratha placed Meera's gift box inside her cupboard and quietly sifted through the pile of other gifts.

Sameira added, "As you wish. Come on now, open my gift." Saying this, she drew her package from the gift pile, handing it over to Pratha. Tearing through the wrapping, Pratha was happy to see a branded makeup kit along with different-sized brushes.

"Wow, this is awesome; I love it," claimed Pratha as she hugged Sameira. The latter remarked, "Now this… is a best friend's gift." There was a strange silence in the room as Pratha quietly processed Sameira's comment.

There were a few knocks on the door. Moments later, Pratha's mother walked in wearing a night suit. Scanning the bedroom, she chuckled, "Ah, a wonderful gift expo here." As she approached Pratha, she held out her mobile phone. "Here, Meera is waiting on the call." Turning to Sameira, she smiled. "Hope you enjoyed your best friend's party."

Sameira: "Yes, it was fun. Sadly, it's all over."

Pratha's mother: "Oh dear… then I have an idea for you both. Tonight, let's make it a sleepover, giving you both more time to be together. What do you say?"

Pratha was excited at the suggestion. But Sameira was in a dilemma. She looked at Pratha. "I would love to stay tonight, but my parents will not approve of last-minute plans. Let us plan for another day. Shall we?" she asked Pratha and her mother doubtfully.

"Yes, of course. You are very sensible, Sameira. I think we should agree with your suggestion. Shall we plan for another day, Pratha?"

"Yes, Mother. Sameira is right. Let's plan it along with Meera."

Sameira: "Ok, great then. My father should be here in some time to pick me up. Meanwhile, let's finish with Meera's call. Right, Pratha?"

Pratha: "Oh yes, in the middle of our conversation, I completely forgot that Meera was waiting on the line. Let's talk to her."

Pratha's mother patted Sameira on the shoulder as she walked away, closing the door behind her.

Meera: "Hey, birthday gal, wishing you a wonderful day again. I hope you liked my gift?"

Pratha: "Yes, of course. Thank you. You know they are my favourite. It's a thoughtful gift. By the way, I was hoping you would stay longer tonight."

Meera: "I know, and I wanted to. But my grandparents were leaving, and I had to rush back earlier than planned. I'm totally missing you both…. Hmm. Tell me, what other gifts did you receive?"

Before Pratha could respond, Sameira grabbed the mobile and turned on the speaker. "Hey Meera, hope you are missing us both… Just for the record, I love 'Ikar' sandals. I am not a fan of the elite brand napkins. Ok?" laughed Sameira loudly.

"Come on, man. Pratha really likes them and is happy about it. So that settles it. What was your gift?" probed Meera.

"A very nice, branded makeup kit. I will use it for the school annual day function," claimed Pratha. There was cheerful laughter on both sides. Soon Sameira's father arrived. As the friends bid goodbye to each other, Sameira headed back home.

It was already the next week, the day of the class test. Sameira and Pratha walked in along with the rest of the students. Meera was already seated in her spot, studying inside the classroom, immersed in her books. The two girls approached and greeted her, but she did not notice them coming. Pratha grabbed the book from the table while Sameira snapped her fingers across Meera's face. Both girls wore a surprised look on their faces, trying to gather Meera's attention. Meera realised she was not alone and that her class was about to begin shortly.

Meera: "Sorry, I didn't see you both coming. I am preparing for today's test. I… I couldn't study over the weekend, so I need some time alone, please."

Sameira asked sarcastically, "Oh, I see. But why?"

Pratha: "Come on, dear. I am sure you will score the most marks." Placing her bag on the desk, Pratha sat beside Meera to her right.

Sameira sat to Meera's left and smiled mischievously. "I agree. But today's test is cancelled, so why are you still revising?" she said, winking at Pratha.

Meera: "Really? Is it not today?" she asked, looking happy.

Pratha: "I wish. But that's a joke," she discerned.

Sameira: "We all had a whole week to prepare. What happened?"

Meera: "I was not in town, and the test slipped off my mind. I remembered only last night while packing for school." She frowned. "I came early this morning and, without the teacher's knowledge, sneaked into the classroom," whispered Meera.

"Wow, that's adventurous. You skipped the prayer meet to study in the classroom! Pratha, we should try this," grinned Sameira. There were giggles among the friends, which caused the class leader to shush them, as students were doing a final review before the test.

The teacher walked in, and students rose to greet her. "Good morning, ma'am." Miss Lily reciprocated, "Good morning. Close all books and settle down. We will start the test," she commanded.

Placing a pile of papers on her table, she added, "You will have 30 minutes to answer ten questions. Pick one paper and pass the rest to the back bench," instructed the teacher as she placed a bundle of answer sheets on the first bench of each row in the room. "Spread out and keep an arm's distance from each other. No talking and copying is strictly unacceptable," continued Miss Lily.

As she jotted down ten questions on the blackboard, the students assumed their positions to start the test. "These are the questions." Looking at her wristwatch, she said, "The test starts now; go on."

Reading the questions one after the other, Meera's worry grew with each passing question on the board. She glanced at Miss Lily, moving around the class and watching over the students. She then looked at Sameira and Pratha, engrossed in writing. Meera bent down and stared hard at the blank paper under her palm. The pen between her fingers wouldn't move. Ten minutes into the test, she grew tense. "A blank paper. How do I hand this in? I need to at least attempt to answer. Otherwise, I will be mocked in front of other students. I need to do something now," she resolved with a heavy heart.

She observed the class teacher's movements. Miss Lily strolled around, watching over the students. As the teacher moved away from her side, Meera took the opportunity and signalled to her friend, gently tapping her hand beside Sameira's paper. Sameira was distracted and looked towards Meera.

"Show me your answers," Meera whispered.

Sameira raised her eyebrows in disbelief. "What?" she whispered back.

"Help me. Show me your answers," Meera gave a pleading look. Sameira understood her request. Drawing a deep breath, she noticed Miss Lily walking towards her and continued writing. As the teacher walked away, Sameira allowed Meera to get a clear view of her answers by adjusting her paper and hand position accordingly.

As time passed, the teacher gave instructions at the end of thirty minutes: "Stop writing and put down your pens." The paper beneath Meera's hand was no longer blank. She was relieved and discreetly thanked Sameira for her help.

The next day, the teacher handed over the evaluated answer papers to all the students. She called Sameira and Meera together to come forward and collect their papers. Meera felt uneasy as their names were called together. Both approached Miss Lily and waited by her side. The teacher handed Meera's paper, which had good marks. She then turned to Sameira and reprimanded her for being dishonest. "Did you not have a week to prepare for the test?" probed Miss Lily.

"Yes, ma'am, I did," responded Sameira, not following her line of questioning.

"Then why did you cheat on the test? Despite my strict instructions, you dared to disobey your teacher. Regardless of my warning, you have still copied from Meera."

Sameira was shocked to hear the accusations hurled at her. She replayed the teacher's words in her mind, trying to grasp the meaning. "Ma'am thinks I copied from Meera, while it is the other way around. What makes her think I did?" she wondered, transfixed.

Meera was shocked by the teacher's claim. Since Miss Lily was conversing with Sameira, Meera dared not interrupt. She patiently awaited her turn to speak.

Meanwhile, Sameira said, "Ma'am, I did not copy during the test. You should ask Meera. I came prepared and did fairly well on the paper."

Miss Lily: "Sameira, you are lying to my face. You think I will not identify copied answers. This is your last chance to come clean; otherwise, I will have to call for a PTM," she warned.

Meera stared hard at Miss Lily and Sameira. As the teacher warned Sameira, Meera's heart skipped a beat. While the conversation grew intense, Meera could not look away from Sameira, watching her closely and capturing every expression on her face.

Sameira assured, "Sorry, ma'am. I am telling the truth; I did not copy." With tears welling up in her eyes, she looked at Meera.

Sameira thought to herself, "Meera is conveniently quiet, not admitting that she copied from me. Even if I tell, will Miss Lily believe that Meera did it?"

Meera interrupted, "Excuse me, ma'am." But her voice was too feeble to interrupt their conversation. She tried again but couldn't gather the teacher's attention out of fear. She quickly ran her palm across her throat, checking if all was well. All seemed fine. She tried speaking again, but her voice was choked with embarrassment and inaudible.

In her head, Meera wondered about her teacher's confidence in her. "Why did ma'am not suspect me of copying? Does she think so highly of me? All this while, regardless of Sameira's denial, ma'am has not accepted that I could have cheated. Certainly, Miss Lily thinks well and considers me good. In reality, poor Sameira has been generous to help me. She is now suffering ma'am's wrath for my mistake. Shouldn't I help Sameira by admitting the truth? Oh, the truth… What a shame! If I speak the truth, my image will be shattered instantly. Sameira will then be safe, but what about me? Miss Lily will never see me the same way as now. She will mock me in front of others. I will lose my studious good image. I wish I didn't have to admit the truth."

Miss Lily: "Sameira, I thought you would accept your mistake and apologise. But you are so stubborn."

Meera continued reflecting, "On the other hand, if I don't support my friend, I will lose her. Her image will be damaged while she has not wronged. This fix has landed both of us in trouble. I cannot save my image, but at least my innocent friend will recover from this problem." Meera resolved to do the unthinkable.

Meera mustered some courage and, reassuring herself repeatedly, she interrupted the teacher. "Apologies, ma'am. I wish to say something."

Miss Lily looked at Meera. "Yes?"

Meera: "Ma'am, Sameira is telling the truth; she did not copy during the test."

Miss Lily: "Is that so? Then did you do it?"

Meera spoke in a composed manner. "Yes, ma'am. Sorry. I did. Last weekend I was out of town and had no time to prepare. I tried my best to revise this morning. Unfortunately, I copied from Sameira without her knowledge."

Miss Lily was taken aback to hear Meera's confession. She stared hard at her. Gathering her thoughts, she spoke in a bitter tone. "Meera, I did not think you would do this. This is unacceptable." The teacher took a long pause and continued, "Since you have confessed, I am not taking action for now. But next time, there will be strict action if I catch you repeating or disobeying." she warned Meera.

Meera assured, "Yes, ma'am. I will not repeat this again. I am extremely sorry."

Looking at Sameira, Miss Lily spoke, "You should have told me about Meera. Next time, speak up. Anyways, you have done well in the test and continue the hard work." She patted Sameira's arm and instructed them to return to their seats.

A strange sense of relief pervaded them both. All that had transpired among the three was too much and too soon. Without all the rumbling, a thunderstorm had passed, carving moral judgements on one another.

Being dishonest in one aspect and brutally honest in another seems a premise for some intellectuals, on a level playing field.

As Miss Lily wrapped up the class, she left with a parting gaze at Meera, reflecting, "not many will dare to speak the truth for the sake of another, undaunted by the consequences. You could marvel someday."

A lot was felt in the silence. Meera held Sameira's hand. "I am sorry you had to go through so much for helping me."

Her eyes still wet, Sameira smiled back at Meera. "Okay, and thanks for telling the truth. Otherwise, Miss Lily may not have believed me."

Meera hugged Sameira. "Thanks for forgiving me." Sameira obliged by wrapping her arms around Meera.

Pratha, watching both her friends, asked, "What's going on? I want a hug too." She flung her arms around Meera and Sameira, embracing them as they hugged each other.

Pratha: "What were you guys discussing, for so long with Miss Lily? The suspense is too much. Fill me in quickly," she demanded.

Both Meera and Sameira laughed softly in response to Pratha's eagerness. Joy-filled giggles swept through the classroom, amid the loud chatter of other students.

BUTTERFLY DISTRESS

The forest buzzed with the sound of activity and wild whispers of nothing. A refreshing late morning shone brightly amid low-hanging juicy fruits, sweet-smelling flowers, lush green plants, and sharp trees. Birds chirped, and fluttering filled the ambience. A monkey wandered, jumping across trees, exploring the forest, wondering what he could do that day.

As he passed a bush of flowery plants, a bunch of colourful butterflies hovered around, looking unusually big in size and of various bright colours: red, blue, green, and yellow. They were quite attractive, and the monkey was enchanted by their appearance. Leaping forward to grab them, he succeeded in catching the yellow butterfly while the others flew away safely.

The yellow butterfly was scared and tried to free itself, but all in vain. The monkey had trapped the yellow butterfly, holding it captive within the circled enclosure of his large palms, held together. The curious monkey peeked through the gap in his palm to catch a glimpse of the trembling beauty.

The devastated yellow butterfly pleaded, "Oh, monkey, you are big and powerful. I am a tiny insect, capable of no use or harm to you. Please let me go."

The monkey was surprised to hear the butterfly speak. He took a decisive look at the insect and said, "I didn't know butterflies could speak. You are special. How can I let you go? Let's hear all that you can say. Amuse me," he commanded.

The poor insect begged for its life while the monkey remained obstinate.

The butterfly continued in a calm tone, "Dear monkey, you are a good friend. I would like to please you, and if you set me free, I will lead you to the banana grove where you can eat an abundance of delicious fruit, all for yourself to relish."

The monkey laughed loudly in disbelief. "Oh, your jokes. What else have you got?" he said in a curious tone, nodding in denial.

The butterfly wouldn't give up and continued to assure the monkey about the feast awaiting at the grove. To win the monkey's favour, he further painted a verbal picture of the low-lying fruits and the huge grove with his sheer talent of articulation. The monkey still couldn't believe how an average butterfly could articulate so well. All the while, a craving was ignited in the monkey's mind.

He thought: what if the butterfly is telling the truth? It is quite possible that an amazing butterfly could know about an extravagant grove. I, too, am not familiar with the forest, and this butterfly is not enough of a meal. Trusting the insect is not a bad idea, as I lose nothing, whereas I stand to gain a delicious meal if the grove is real.

The monkey agreed to the deal. The moment it opened its palm, the butterfly instantly flew and, in split seconds, was out of sight. The monkey lost track of the desperate butterfly. It was gone.

He sensed deception on the part of the butterfly and grew angry. "Oh! What a dreadful insect. It made a fool of me. I shall avenge this deceit," he grumbled, looking at his empty palm.

As the monkey walked a few steps, he passed a bush. Noticing three colourful butterflies hovering over the flowers, he remembered the yellow butterfly. It was nowhere around. The monkey leapt forward to catch them. He turned lucky and caught the blue butterfly this time.

The shocked blue butterfly spoke thus, "Oh, dear monkey. I have done you no harm, so please let me go. I shall lead you to the apple grove. I shall live another day while you can feast on delicious apples."

The monkey rebuked the butterfly, "No, you won't. You would rather fly away, for I will eat you now."

The butterfly was petrified and promised to keep its word. Tempted by thoughts of the delicious apples, the monkey reluctantly agreed to the deal. He freed the butterfly and remained alert, following it closely. They reached a river, and the blue butterfly flew over the flowing water. The monkey was hesitant to enter the river and stood on the riverbank, stranded on one shore, while the apple grove was on the other shore. Left behind, the hapless monkey watched the blue butterfly fly farther away and eventually out of sight. The monkey was disheartened. Dropping his shoulders, he turned back and took a few steps. He looked back to catch a glimpse of the blue butterfly; alas, it was nowhere to be seen. The monkey grew suspicious of the butterfly's intent. He decided to vent his anger on any butterfly he encountered. He drew up a plan to avenge the mistreatment meted to him. As he walked past a flowerless plant, he noticed a green butterfly resting on a leaf. The monkey succeeded in holding it captive.

The insect did not protest and spoke calmly: "Oh! Dear monkey. I see you are tired. Would you like to eat some fresh juicy oranges? I am headed to the orange grove that is not far from here."

The monkey was hungry and angry, too. He said, "Instead of the oranges, you look delicious and mouthful.

My experience tells me to live in this moment rather than run after a grove that is further away." At that point, he opened his mouth and loosened his grip on the insect to swallow the green butterfly. Taking this opportunity, the butterfly slipped away, startling the monkey.

As the green butterfly flew, it spoke: "Come on, monkey. The orange grove is nearby." Commanding so, the insect flew in the opposite direction. A few miles and the orange grove would be visible. The monkey was excited. He thought, "Third time's a charm. Finally, I am reaching the grove without being deceived by the tricky butterfly."

Along the way, there was quicksand. The insect flew over it, but the monkey was unable to jump or cross over. He needed to detour. He took some time to replan his way. But before he could communicate with the green butterfly, it was almost on the other side of the land beyond the quicksand. Unable to keep track of the butterfly, the monkey took the easy way out—give up and sulk. He walked away with his head hanging low and tears welling up in his eyes, exhausted from his unfulfilled pursuits to reach the juicy groves.

Wiping his eyes, he then jumped across branches towards someplace safe. A red butterfly hovered around him. Without a second thought, the disinterested monkey settled on a branch and ignored the unwelcome company.

The red butterfly enquired, "Monkey, aren't you hungry? I am surprised that the grove was not enticing enough for you. Were the hurdles on your way impossible to cross?"

The monkey replied in a bitter tone, "The butterflies fooled me, using my weakness to their advantage. I gave them back their lives, not once but thrice. Regardless, these cheaters did not look out for me but blatantly lied and presented me with false hopes. Leading me to the grove was a veil of deception for these selfish brutes. They have hurt me deeply."

The red butterfly said, "Oh, monkey, I pity you. You freed them in good faith, and now it is you who is feeling desolate. Can I ask you something?"

The monkey frowned and nodded.

The red butterfly asked, "Had you pursued the path relentlessly, would you have still felt the same?"

The monkey replied, "Of course. It's not about me. It's about them. The flies have wronged me."

The red butterfly said, "How?... can flies ensure a monkey's path is scalable?"

(silence)

"Apart from eating delicious juicy fruits, did you plan or attempt to reach the groves by yourself? Was it not agreed that the flies would lead you to the grove, and they indeed did so?"

The monkey was offended. "How dare you accuse me? I am still hurting because of the likes of you!" The monkey fumed in anger.

The red butterfly was quick to say, "I am sorry for your pain. Trust me, I have no intent to cause you harm. But if you could allow me, I can explain that my words are only aimed at easing your suffering. All this pain and anger that you sense within yourself may feel pointless when you understand the premise. If you wish to engage in generous listening and with a receptive mind, we can establish the stemming point of your disappointment. Are you inclined to try, monkey?"

The monkey replied, "You are crueller to me than others. I have not invited you to preach to me. Leave me alone," said the emotionally devastated monkey.

The red butterfly said, "Agreed. I came to work with you, to help you heal sooner. But as you wish, it can take a long time to process your bitter feelings, all by yourself. Perhaps a quick addressal, will need courage on your part. It will be, to rise above your urge for an immediate win and delve into a long-term big emotional win. Perhaps your choice is also for the best. I shall take my leave," said the red butterfly in a soft monotonic tone.

The monkey asked, "What... courage? I know what is best for me. I will show you my courage by smashing you in the blink of an eye." He then repeatedly swung his arm at the red butterfly. But the butterfly was quick to evade every attempt. The monkey was exhausted and gave up.

Panting for breath, he took a long stare at the red butterfly and spoke, "You are an expert at this. You are playing games with me, aren't you? What else have you got? Go on, I am listening to you."

The red butterfly smiled. "Dear monkey, thank you. You have done well for both of us. Let us first understand your problem. We all get emotional based on our perception of ourselves and others. Your sense of self-pity leads to thinking that all which transpired is betrayal, leaving you emotionally burdened. If you take a moment to empathise with the butterflies, you may see them as honest and within fair reason. Perhaps your sense of vengeance will vanish. Decisions that hold well in one situation are not necessarily good in another. If you make an effort to interpret the events from a wider perspective, bring both sides together, your emotions can shift to a place of ease, and you shall certainly feel better."

The monkey was dumbfounded. He slowly gathered his thoughts. It was difficult to shift perspective. He needed to feel secure, and only then could he consider the other side of the event. He thus spoke: "Courage is essential to overcome my fear of being insignificant. It feels nice to be important. But giving importance to another over oneself is very hard, as if killing one's self-interest." Regardless, how do you come by all this information about me? I have not interacted with you before and am seeing you only now.

The red butterfly replied, "I have been by your side and observing you all this while. You trapped my friends and forced them to abide by you. Not once did the thought cross your mind that it is also important to be nice to others, those taking care of your needs and well-being. How thankless!"

The monkey ignored the butterfly's judgement. He focused on calmly introspecting the event. "The yellow butterfly did tell me to follow it. As I was not pressed by hunger, I took it lightly and missed following the butterfly. The reason for missing the banana grove is not all on the yellow butterfly. The blue butterfly took me over a river stream. I was unprepared to cross over. Had I acted with the presence of mind using a log or by swimming, I may have reached the apple grove. Again, the blue butterfly may not be all to blame. With the green butterfly, I made no effort to cross the quicksand to reach the orange grove. I may have failed to rise above lethargy and engage in timely action. As a consequence, I feel unfulfilled and hungry while listening to this boring red butterfly," he frowned.

The red butterfly continued, "Monkey, have you thought through today's happenings? What happened?"

The monkey nodded in denial, his eyes lowered.

The red butterfly continued, "Firstly, you were unprepared for the pursuit. Second, your emotions clouded your judgement and undermined your opportunity. Third, prejudice prevents you from accomplishing your goal. Your dedicated efforts would have definitely saved the day for you. A positive perspective is key to winning or losing opportunities. I hope you will shape your own path to success and not chase others to serve it to you." The red butterfly moved away.

Hearing all this, the monkey felt drawn towards and chased the red butterfly, calling out, "I have one last question. You shall answer me, right?"

"Yes," replied the pleased red butterfly.

"By now, I have understood that you love preaching. But why me? Tell me, how do you know all this about me?"

The red butterfly said, "I am your mind. I know everything about you." Saying so, it vanished into thin air.

GREEN WISH

Anew commercial complex stood in the place of once empty land, that had been ridden with dirt and immobile vehicles, either parked, shredded, or stolen by scrap sellers.

Veena is 15 years old, studying at the 'Prathamik Vidyalaya' in the garden city of the state. Her daily commute to school involves walking about a mile each way. Ensuring to start early from home, she walks leisurely to her school and back. Along the way, her pastime is to watch and admire the freshly bloomed flowers and brightly standing trees lined up on either side of the street. Gradually, she found nature's beauty to be far more engaging. When she noticed alluring flowers, she would stop to observe them closely, as if studying their attributes while admiring them— "Wow, these refreshingly colourful flowers are so appealing. Their abundant beauty and fragrance make watching and being around them joyful." Thinking through her day's activities, she walked past the huge Tabebuia rosea positioned in the centre of her street. Having crossed it, she realised the absence of the vast canopy that marked her route, serving as a landmark to everyone around.

"Oh… I missed my turn and am heading in the wrong direction," she mumbled to herself, retracing her path and taking a turn at the beautiful Tabebuia rosea tree. A few more steps and she reached her home. Recounting the happenings, she reflected —"When watching plants and trees, I simply lose my way. But why?.... because I like engaging with them. Maybe I can do something interesting with this hobby... Hmm, should I turn this into a study subject? Perhaps learn about the flora?" she wondered and thus resolved.

Two days later, she carried a handbook containing pictures and notes about flowers and fruits. She hoped to make good use of her pastime. As she walked by an interesting flower or tree, she would swiftly go through the pages in the book, to identify them. Over time, she memorised them all. That afternoon, as Veena reached home later than usual, her mother, Rama, was worried and irritated.

"Veena, what took you so long? Was there any problem at school or on the way?" she inquired.

Hugging her mother from behind, Veena replied, "Mother, I learned about four new flowers on the way home. Did you know all flowers have a scientific name? Jasmine is called 'jasminum,' rose is 'rosa rubiginosa,' hibiscus is 'rosa sinensis,' and shevanti is 'chrysanthemum indicum.' They all have varieties ranging from hundreds to several thousands. Each of them is beautiful and smells very different from the others."

Releasing her hold, Rama gently probed, "At school?"

Turning around and walking away, Veena replied, "On my way to school and back home."

In the following months, she developed a good knowledge in her area of interest and was happy about her new hobby.

It was mid-year, and the time for the annual science exhibition at school. Each student came up with a scientific presentation of their choice. As for Veena, the choice was obvious—an elaborate 3D presentation of the plant life cycle. All students submitted their presentations for evaluation.

That Sunday, at the breakfast table, Veena's father, Viren, inquired, "Veena, how is the science exhibition coming along? Tell me all about it."

Eager to share, Veena was excited. "Appa, the exhibition went well. My concept was a plant life cycle in a 3D model.

I also did a second exhibit along with my friends. That too is a 3D model. Our teachers have appreciated them both."

Viren said, "Hmm, excellent. Have you already submitted them, or can I still see them?"

Veena replied, "Before submission, I tried showing you on a video call but couldn't connect with you."

Viren said, "Yes, I remember. I was travelling on work. No worries. I saw the pictures. They are good, and I can always see them once you bring them home, right?"

Veena frowned and said, "Sorry, Appa, my exhibit is among the top five selected for the school annual day display. I can bring it only after a fortnight; not sure what condition it will be in by then."

Rama said, "Congratulations that your work is selected, but what will they do with it for so long?"

Viren asked, "How about your group exhibit?"

Veena replied, "Top exhibits will be displayed on the stage in the main hall during the annual day celebrations. We will also be awarded the winning certificates. Meanwhile, let me tell you about our group display. The theme is a proxy version of 'My Green City.' It's a 3D model of plush greenery, water bodies, and landmark buildings of our city. We have showcased a lower carbon footprint in our city compared to neighbouring ones. Since only individual exhibits are eligible, our group exhibit does not qualify for selection. Regardless, our idea and effort were greatly applauded by our principal and others. You would see that it's relevant in current times," she smiled.

Nodding and smiling in agreement, Viren and Rama were elated at their daughter's attitude and accomplishment.

Later that morning, they watched on television as the 'City Commercial Centre' was inaugurated by the mayor. Addressing the crowd from the newly ordained convention centre, the mayor spoke at the event, "Today we are creating history as we inaugurate the largest commercial centre in our country, right here in our city. This centre houses several commercial structures for administrative and public utility, including a large shopping complex, multiple convention and entertainment facilities, healthcare, and many more attractions. It will serve as a one-stop shop for all purposes, capable of accommodating one-third of the city's crowd at a given time. I welcome all of you to come and avail the spacious indoor and outdoor facilities of our new commercial centre."

Journalist: "Congratulations, Mr. Mayor. This is fantastic. What have you planned next for our city?"

Mayor: "We have large-scale, very interesting endeavours coming up next. Our vision for our city is to implement a well-planned infrastructure. First of all, we will widen and lay new roads for all-round accessibility. Secondly, we will build commercial towers across the city to house corporate and commercial business growth. These will pave the way for our economic boost, given the expansion and growth opportunities in the near future."

The media and audience cheered, and the sound of claps echoed all over the complex.

Veena and her parents keenly watched the telecast. "Good work; this shall bring in new employment opportunities for all," remarked Viren.

Veena observed, "How about carbon emissions? I did not hear anything about environmental protection all along."

Viren noted, "I am sure the environment welfare committee will take cognizance of such large-scale developments in the city. The impact on the city's ecological condition is no joke."

Veena looked concerned and commented, "The other day, while returning from school, I saw some workers clearing the sidewalks. I thought they were cleaning, but it looked like they were bringing them down. How about the trees and plants along the street and large open spaces?"

Rama patted Veena's back. "You don't need to worry about all this. Pick up your books and focus on studying. You have assignments to complete," reminded Rama. Veena nodded in agreement but couldn't take her mind off the upcoming changes to the city's infrastructure.

Her concern grew valid over the coming weeks. Trees were being cut down, and space was being made for extending roads and building structures. Veena sometimes watched the scene along the roads during her commute. It greatly bothered her that huge trees were gone within hours and in their place stood nothing but dust and empty space awaiting the dominance of concrete structures.

Seeing this sight, Veena mumbled, "Will my city remain a paradise or become home to dust and dryness?" She penned a heartfelt note that night on her social media handle. It read, "Tabebuia rosea, my pink trumpet, stood right at the entrance of our street." A welcoming arch, alluring us with the beautiful flower show, she took all under her cooling shade, never discriminating. I loved to stand beneath her, and Dad would shake off a low-lying branch, surprising me with a flower shower. I loved it the first time. I loved it every time we did it for fun. From ruling our hearts and spreading cheer, to being nature's landmark. I miss her, every time I turn onto my street on my way home. With a hard smile and teary eyes, I now bid adieu at the spot where she stood for ages but not anymore. As all things, good and bad, come to an end, my pink trumpet among so many wonderful oldies has left to make way for a new world around me.

I wonder, why should our beloved good things come to an end? Can't we have the new and fancy while retaining our age-old goodness? Why isn't this logical?

Me with my pink trumpet and… Those happy times ☺"

By the next evening, her post had garnered several hundred likes and reposts. Some comments read, "True that, I am so touched by your connection to a tree you grew up watching. We too miss ours, but as time flies, things change, making way for new life."

Other comments read, "We share your thoughts. Not sure if this is ideal for our future and our city."

"Move on… You can always get another one," and so on.

During the school break, Veena was quiet, watching other students playing around. The playground was surrounded by large trees and plants. She felt lively despite the scorching heat outside.

That evening, she posted again on her social media handle, "Friends, century-old trees and plants stand, looking over my school playground. All this within the secured gates of our school premises. Likewise, to keep our city green, we too need to secure and guard our biodiversity. I pledge to plant two saplings for every tree cut from my street. What do you think? Would you also join me in my pledge?" To her post, she tagged her friends and the city mayor's official page.

Over the next week, her post garnered thousands of likes and hundreds of reposts. Overwhelming as it was to receive such huge support, she, along with her family and friends, launched a social media campaign to spread the word: "Plant trees, not cut."

She and her friends began a silent campaign for the cause. Whether at school or stepping out of their homes, wherever they went, they wore their slogans on them. Their clothes and bags had slogans pinned, loud and bold.

Several students from the school joined them in the campaign by sporting slogans on their bags and accessories. The quiet campaign began to spread across students and their networks too. The school management was cognizant and did not approve. The class teacher convened a meeting with the principal and the campaigning group of students.

The teacher instructed, "While the agenda of your campaign may be directed at a vital social cause, it is not acceptable within the school premises. Students are required to strictly adhere to the protocols and cannot practise any campaigns during school hours. What you have done disturbs the decorum and goes too far. Discipline is utmost in school premises. This may appear as a calm campaign, but we cannot permit the display of these slogans on your bags, and accessories. You are required to leave these outside before entering the school premises."

Veena: "Apologies Madam. Our intent was to spread awareness about our environment. We thought a speechless campaign would not be a troublemaker or inconvenience to anybody. Without disturbing any routine, we wanted to emphasise the conservation of our green city before it's too late."

The principal intervened, "You are all here to study, build knowledge, and grow as good individuals. Campaigning for social causes is not in your curriculum and should not be your agenda. These activities digress student attention from the purpose of systemic education. We have clearly explained what the school expects from the students. You are not permitted to continue this during school hours. Feel free to do what you wish outside school premises in your personal time. We have made it very clear, and there is no room for more discussion on this topic."

The teacher added, "All of you should immediately remove the banners pinned to your person and items. Any disobedience will be dealt with strict disciplinary action, leading up to suspension with immediate effect."

The students were shocked to hear the warning and quickly apologised. Doing away with all that was to be, they went back to their classrooms. There was a sense of emptiness among the group of friends after obeying the school management.

Veena and her friends were seated at the back bench. The science teacher entered the class. Before starting, she noticed the campaign group was seated together. Intending to break their moods, she commanded them to de-group and spread across the classroom.

After school hours, the group met and discussed at the playground.

Veena was complaining, "I am disappointed by what happened today. We are not allowed to carry on a calm, quiet campaign for environmental causes? This is not working. It's difficult to wrap my head around this. Our technique was effective, and the management also witnessed the impact. Had we been given a chance to continue, we would have garnered more and more support from most of the students. It's disheartening how environmental causes are shoved under the pretext of rules. Now our cause can't reach far and wide."

Prashanth: "Are you serious? For the sake of campaigning, we cannot risk suspension from school. It's true the management saw the effectiveness. Maybe they wanted to maintain control over students, and so, before it was out of their control, they took strong measures to curtail us and the other students."

From what happened today, it tells me we are headed in the right direction. We should now balance our studies and the campaign. If our parents learn of the warning we received today, they will not support our campaign initiative. Let us be careful not to offend anybody while proceeding to plan our next steps. Yeah?"

Bry: "I agree with both of you. We should certainly not stop here. But outside school hours, we have our homework and studies too. We will not be left with much time for the environmental cause. What else can we do to balance our priorities? In fact, we need to solve this issue soon, or all our efforts put in so far will be wasted. We will reach nowhere, and our initiative will die out," Bry frowned.

Sureka: "I get it. Hearing all of you, I can think of only one solution. What we did inside the school, we should repeat outside the school too."

Bry: "Come on, Sureka, we are already doing that. It's nothing new. Don't you hear me? We don't have time for outside activities."

Sureka: "I did. Please hear me out fully before jumping in. We should now take our cause to each person individually. We need to think of a method in which every person can be involved in the environmental cause to preserve our green city. But the question is, how do we achieve this? All we need is an idea to enable everybody to participate in our cause."

Manaswini asked hesitantly, "Hmm… How about making seed balls? Everybody can grow plants and trees. We can learn this ourselves and educate others too. This will be taking our cause to each person individually, right? Will this fit our plan?"

Veena was excited, "Excellent. Let's do seed balls. That will solve all the problems that each of us is raising. We can sell them online to fund our cause. Also, we can undertake a plantation drive with the help of our family and friends. What do you say, friends? Shall we embark on this… hmm… our project?"

Bry, standing with his hands inside his pants pockets, "That sounds about right. We can set timelines and start the work… hmm… Seems doable to me. What do others have to say?" Grinning at his friends, he shrugged approvingly.

All of them looked at each other, a slow hesitant smile playing on all their lips and their eyes brightening up. "Yeah, yes… Let's do it," they spoke in unison. Cheers sounded in the playground.

Prashanth: "Let's call it our 'Green Project.' Yeah?"

Veena: "Our 'Green Wish Project.' How does that sound?"

All others: "Yeah, the Green Wish Project." Some laughed, while others jumped and nodded in agreement.

Early that evening, soon after school, Veena discussed during the family's tea break: "Amma, Appa, I want to join a group study with my friends. We plan to meet daily for two hours, at one of our houses, and change places every week. Shall I plan our place for this week's study?" she asked.

"Sure, when are you starting? I need advance notice to prepare edibles for you all," smiled Rama.

"Is it the same group from your science exhibition?" probed Viren.

"Yes, yes, same. We will start studying from today. They should be here in an hour's time," replied Veena with a mischievous smile and an innocent gaze. Her parents were astonished.

"So, all this conversation was only to inform us, not to seek our permission, right?" remarked Viren.

"Let's say, pretending to seek our permission at the last minute," remarked Rama sharply.

"Sorry, but… I really want to…" smiled Veena sheepishly, blinking her innocent eyes repeatedly at them both. They stared at her for a moment.

Rama, with a smirk, nodded approvingly. "Okay."

The stage was set. Veena's interest in plants was evolving to a whole new level. Boys and girls brought the materials required for the seed balls. Seeds of several flowering and fruit-bearing plants and trees were segregated into various tiny packets. Occasionally, Veena was in the habit of making seed balls for gifting purposes. This time, the purpose was environmental. Time flew, and 150 seed balls were ready to dry by late evening. At the end of the first gathering, the outcome was gratifying. Their motivation grew every day, adding to another fruitful day.

By the third day, they were experts and progressing well. It was time to embark on the second step—'disclose and advertise' on social media handles: "Hey friends, we are flora enthusiasts. We have some plans for environmental preservation. Would you like to join us? Yes? Great. Seed ball distribution and plantation drive are coming up very soon. Keep watching this space and come back here soon, for more."

The target audience was friends, acquaintances, extended families, and neighbours. Internally, they conducted all parents' virtual conference meet, to discuss their Green Wish initiative. The idea was loved by most of the audience, while a few others were neutral. Parents encouraged the students and assisted them by providing necessary networks for conducting the drive.

By the fifth day, invites were sent to the target audience through social media handles, calls, messages, and word of mouth. By the week's close, more than a thousand seed balls were dried and ready.

The drive was at a nearby garden park on Sunday morning. The time was chosen well to engage a large public audience, including the regular park-goers. The garden park covered a huge area of land.

Viren and Rama, along with the other eager parents, stood holding banners and loudspeakers. The cloth banner read: "Plant trees, not cut." The leading group gave a speech.

Bry: "Good morning, all. We are the students of Class 9. We all learn in school that plants and trees conserve our environment. They are essential for the upkeep of our soil, climate, water, and overall our planet Earth. So…"

Sureka: "We have gathered here today to plant seeds and grow more trees for our future." Looking at her group members, she continued, "Friends, can you tell me how to conserve my environment? Is there a plan?"

Prashanth: "Oh yes, let me help you. Behind where we stand, there is a large open space with thinly populated greenery. Here, all the action will happen today." Looking at his group members, he continued, "Friends, can you tell me how all this will transpire now?"

Manaswini: "Yes, of course. Seed balls are where the magic happens. We are providing seed balls here. All of the audience is urged to please participate in today's planting drive. We urge the audience to come forward and collect seed balls from our volunteers. Our volunteers are standing by the banners. We request each of the participants to collect up to five balls." Looking at her group members, she continued, "Friends, what are we required to do with the seed balls?"

Sureka: "Oh yes, the dispersal is very important. Carrying the seed balls, please walk through the vast area behind us, where you can scatter them as you like, far and wide. After you scatter them, please water your seed balls. Isn't that simple?"

A large crowd of onlookers gathered around them. The activity was simple and fun. A large group of people participated in the drive. After a few hours, all the seed balls were scattered. People carrying personal bottles easily watered their seed balls, while others borrowed or purchased water from nearby sources.

Prashanth: "Thank you all for the participation. We have successfully scattered more than 1000 seed balls with your help. This is huge. Friends, do you know what can be even bigger than today's successful drive?"

Bry: "Tell me, friend. Wait… wait. I can guess… the trees growing out of these seed balls, right? Dear participants, whenever you visit this park, please water your seed balls every day so they can grow well and soon."

Sureka: "Friends, I have a very good feeling from participating in today's green drive. I wish I could do more to conserve my planet. Can I give back more to my environment and not let go?"

Veena: "Sure, there will be more opportunities to secure our ecosphere. Next week, Sunday morning, at the same time and same location as today, we have a drive to make seed balls right here. So, I'm requesting everybody to please attend and participate. Next Sunday, help us make thousands of seed balls. Please bring your friends and family to the drive. This is for us, our future, our city, our home on Earth. Thank you all. Have a fun Sunday."

Many photos and videos of the drive were posted on the social media handles of friends, family, and participants too. They tagged their school and the city civic authorities in their posts.

The next day at school, during the prayer assembly, the principal called upon the Green Wish group to the dais. She announced the grand success of the Green Wish drive and how she too participated in it. Bry, Veena, Prashanth, Sureka, and Manaswini were pleasantly surprised. Standing beside the principal, they received standing ovations from the audience—students and school authorities. The principal was very impressed with the green initiative and announced a semi-annual programme for making seed balls, an activity for high school students. Cheering and claps echoed at the assembly.

The focused effort and hard work of the students paved the way for action-driven awareness. This was the need of the hour as the city embarked on a massive journey of urbanisation, shifting from a green-centric approach to concretisation.

We all thrive for a life of comfort and convenience. To last longer, it is essential to evaluate our choices to this end. Our priorities today will affect our chances of survival tomorrow. In the long run, all species should flourish and not prioritise one, over and above the survival of others. Only if our Earth thrives with a pleasant, conducive atmosphere can our pursuits succeed, ensuring that our species, alongside other life forms, will continue to occupy this planet for a very long time to come.

CATCH ME IF YOU CAN

It was a vibrant summer. All things bright and sharp. Flowers bloomed and dried by the next noon. Thirst and sweat dominated the mindful atmosphere, sporting an unsettled silence.

A ten-story building overlooked the street market. Dance classes in block two would go on during the day. Smelling fresh, girls and boys in crisp clothes walked across the gated community. Soft chatter and loud laughter filled the building foyer. The holiday spirit reigned upon the bouts of life around.

Amid the cheerful exchange of people within the community and the loud chaotic streets of the market, a huge thundering noise struck the ground between the two blocks of the building. Passersby were shocked at the crash and looked around to find two big suitcases lying on the floor. Two guards of the building rushed to the spot, and people surrounded the scene to witness the incident.

An old couple hurried to the spot through the staircase section. Their swift gait, grey hair, and stained, messy clothes elucidated their position. The lady smelled of spices and her fingertips were smeared with turmeric. The old man's shirt was wet on the chest, sleeves rolled up and marked with black dirt. Their facial expressions were of distress. Sweat dripped off the man's face, while tears welled up in the woman's eyes. Their pitiful condition moved the onlookers. By now, a relatively large crowd had assembled at the spot.

As the couple headed straight to the suitcase to secure the baggage lying on the ground, some contents of one broken case had spilled out. They worked together to gather and put back the contents into the suitcase. There was loud chatter among the crowd surrounding them.

Resident 1: "Oh my goodness, did the suitcase actually come down flying from the top floor?"

Resident 2: "Yes, somebody must have thrown them. I wonder who could do this?"

Resident 3: "These flying suitcases are big. It could have fallen on anybody standing or passing by this area. Is anybody hurt?"

Resident 1: "No one was around here. Luckily, nobody was hurt; else it could have been fatal."

Resident 2: "Does the suitcase belong to the old couple? Why did they throw it down?"

Resident 4: "They are old; they couldn't have lifted and hurled these, especially across the balcony. Look how they are struggling to put them together. Somebody young and strong must be the culprit."

Resident 1 & 2: "Possible, but we can't be sure. Let us hear what the old couple has to say."

Resident 3: "We need to inquire, and a formal police complaint is necessary."

Resident 4: "Let's find out. Come on."

Few residents rushed towards the old man and initiated a conversation with him. Meanwhile, the old lady was inconsolable as she sat beside the suitcase and continued to weep incessantly. The old man was not perturbed by her sobs and went about trying to fix the broken handle of the suitcase. He tied it together with a new handkerchief that he pulled out of his pants pocket.

The onlookers grew concerned, and it was apparent that the suitcase belonged to the old couple, since nobody else came looking for the flying boxes. The security and residents were concerned about the unusual happenings and began to inquire with the old couple about who and which flat they were living in.

A few stepped forward to help the couple while simultaneously questioning them about the unusual events unfolding in the vicinity. The security guards refused to help any further without a detailed background of the couple. One resident offered them some water and a seat to sit. There was no reply from the old couple; they were lost in their own discussion.

The old man looked visibly disturbed; all the same, he seemed to disregard his pain and the crowd around him. He softly addressed the old woman as such: "Get up and let us leave. There is nothing left of us here. We can take care of ourselves. And I am still capable of providing for us. Stop weeping for the brats who do not care about your tears. Come on."

The old lady looked around and took a deep breath; in a shaken voice, she spoke: "I cannot believe they threw us out of our house, that too in this manner. This is very humiliating. Why am I alive, to see all this happen to me?"

The old man, standing beside the lady and tapping on her shoulders, said: "Do not think of them anymore. They are not our children. We are for each other, and this is our world now. It is difficult but let us forget about them. They have long forgotten us."

Hearing this, the woman was inconsolable. He wiped her tears with the loose end of her saree. She slowly gathered herself and stood up to leave. A couple of men and women approached them and interrupted: "Uncle, aunty, tell us what is all this that's happening? We shall help you. Did you throw these suitcases from above? Who threw you out of your house? Which flat are you from?"

The security guard queried: "Sir, Madam, which flat do you live in? What happened, is it a family fight? You can tell us, and we will help you. Would you like to talk to the society manager before recording any complaint?"

Regardless of all that people were saying, the man was clearly shaken and stared into the wind. As he recollected the happenings so far, tears welled up in his eyes. After some time, he regained his awareness. People were staring at him, some with pity, some with anger, while others were confused about both of their silence and waiting for a reply.

He tried to speak, but his voice choked with emotions. While trying to step forward, he stumbled. The guard and the association president standing beside him quickly grabbed him by the shoulder, thus securing him from a fall. The old man looked confused and unable to reconcile with reality.

The anxious woman rushed to his side and wailed: "My husband is very disturbed now. Please do not ask questions about what just happened to us. You all have already seen all that transpired. Please do not make us relive and speak of the horror we are suffering. I only have my husband; I cannot lose him," she continued her loud cry.

A few women from the crowd tried to console her: "Aunty, we are here to help you. If you tell us what happened, we will help you. You seem to be new in our society and we haven't met before. We understand it is a difficult time for you. We all feel sorry. You can trust us."

The desolate old woman said: "OK, I will tell. Since I am not familiar with most of you, I am not comfortable sharing our personal problems in this manner." She then turned to the security guards and requested: "I will share details of the issue with the guards. It seems reasonable to discuss with them rather than strangers."

The security guards agreed. While some onlookers protested about the public nuisance that was created and the drama unfolding, they demanded an explanation and details of action to ensure there were no problems created for other residents. Agreeing to this, key members of the society association insisted on staying back with the guards to sort out the issue. Meanwhile, the guards had the old man seated on a chair by the main gate, beside the compound wall. The couple was offered water to drink, and a crowd of onlookers was cleared and requested to leave. The mended suitcase was placed beside the old man.

In a concerned tone, security personnel assured the man about resolving the issue, given their flat number. While the old man's face was turning pale, he was sweating heavily on his face and neck. Feeling uneasy, he leaned to the left, gripping his chest with his right hand and moaning in pain. His wife and others around noticed the change in his behaviour and sensed a looming grave condition. He gradually fell off the chair onto the ground. His head rested on the floor, writhing and moaning in pain.

His frightened wife pulled a mobile phone out of the man's pocket and sat beside him. Placing his head on her lap, she appraised one Mr. Akash about the situation over a phone call. She then resumed dabbing the sweat off the man's face with the loose end of her saree. He appeared to be in a lot of pain and very exhausted. She assured him: "Oh dear, help is on the way. Please bear with me for a short while. Akash will soon be here to drive us to the hospital."

The president of the association offered to drive them to a nearby hospital, but the frightened woman declined the stranger's offer. The security guard offered to call an ambulance, but the woman again declined as she could not afford the cost due to her economic condition.

Within five minutes, a white sedan car arrived and stopped beside the couple. A young man in his mid-thirties hurried from behind the wheel, leaving the driver's door open as he ran towards the old couple. He had a thick moustache and long eyebrows. Wearing formal clothes, he appeared to be shocked upon witnessing the old couple. He spoke: "Aunty, what is all this? Uncle, I am here. You will soon be fine, and we are heading to the hospital now." The old woman requested the guards to help her load the luggage into the car boot. The security initially denied but then obliged reluctantly. The association members enquired with the young man.

Introducing himself to the people around, he said: "I am Akash. They are my family friends. Where is Suresh? I don't see him?" He enquired in a concerned tone. Without waiting for an answer, he went about helping the old man get into the back seat of the sedan.

"Suresh has done this to us. He threw us out of our house. We should hurry to the hospital," she commanded.

The lady occupied the seat beside the wheel while the old man lay still in the back seat. Akash was standing beside the driver's seat, ready to board the car.

Before letting go, the security enquired with him: "What is the flat number and contact details?"

Hurrying all the while, Akash replied: "Silver 215," and shared a mobile number. "You can contact me on this for further details. Please do not bother them in such a delicate condition," he requested.

The society president noted the number and dialled a call. Akash's mobile rang, and the president acknowledged the exchange, saying: "Keep me informed about his condition. We need their personal details and stay in touch."

Akash nodded in agreement and hurried to the driving seat.

As the guards and the society members looked on, the car picked up speed within seconds. As the car crossed over the street, Akash removed a chip from his mobile and cast it out of the window. The car vanished into the air.

The security guards informed their supervisor of the happenings. Association members, along with the guards, discussed the sequence of events. Failing to establish contact with Akash and the old couple, they notified the police station as a precautionary measure.

Thirty minutes into the incident, a police constable arrived from a nearby police station. The incident was narrated to him, and he reviewed the events in sequence. The constable found Akash's mobile switched off and no updates about the hospitalisation. He, along with the guards and association members, headed to flat Silver 215, planning to inquire and notify Suresh, the resident, about the developments so far.

The main door of the flat was locked. Repeated bell rings and knocks went unanswered. After deliberation, the president called Suresh over their community living tool. Repeated calls went unanswered. As they walked towards the lift, they sensed something fishy. The main door to Silver 219 was half open. They walked to the flat wanting to run a quick check with the residents. Again, the doorbell rings went unanswered. The constable pushed open the main door to take a peek inside.

Nobody was to be seen in the hallway and living area. The association members, accompanied by the guards and the constable, walked in. The flat was furnished and appeared to be occupied by a family. The strange quietness around the house was dubious as the constable walked beyond the dining area towards the bedrooms. Accompanied by his retinue, he witnessed the scene of a ransack. All things were hurled around, with no space to step their foot on. The cupboards and lockers were cut open using tools, probably a machine saw. It was a scene of rampage.

All of them looked around over and over again. The worst came true.

The constable spoke in a composed manner: "This is burglary." The guards and association members looked at each other, eyes and mouths wide open. They were transfixed.

The president and other members approached the constable and spoke: "Sir, Silver 215 appears to be unoccupied. We doubt if the old couple was living in that flat with their son, as they claimed. Is it possible that some outsiders are behind all this? Do you see any connection between the old couple and this burglary?"

The constable rushed out of the flat and rang the neighbouring flats' doorbells. They went unanswered. One flat was latched from the outside. They opened the latch to enter the house. To their surprise, this, too, was burgled in a similar manner. A third flat was vacant, with only carpentry work ongoing.

The constable replied: "I don't get a good feeling about this old couple you mention. Are you sure they are not imposters? If they are, they could be the culprits."

He called the police station: "Inspector Sir, the association reported a family dispute involving a resident couple. However, the flat is vacant and unoccupied. Meanwhile, on the same floor, two other flats were burgled, possibly last night or this morning. This seems to be a case of fraud and burglary. Can you please come to the crime scene? Thank you, Sir." He then disconnected the call.

Turning to the guards, the constable instructed: "Seal all the entry and exit points. The inspector will arrive shortly to investigate."

Catch me if you can!

Oh! Creator of the Universe…

Evoke my strengths to transcend my flaws,

so I reach your shores of perfection,

while all persist within me.